HUMAN DESIGN FOR COACHES AND COURSE CREATORS

THE STRATEGY AND ENERGY OF HD IN YOUR BUSINESS

CARMEN FARRELL-KNAPP

CONTENTS

BOOK ONE
REFLECTORS

BOOK TWO
MANIFESTORS

BOOK THREE
PROJECTORS

BOOK FOUR
GENERATORS AND MANIFESTING GENERATORS

HOW TO USE THIS BOOK

HELLO AND WELCOME!

I'm Carmen. It is an honor and a pleasure to know you are reading this. Human Design was the key for me in many ways: business, relationships, money, and spirit. I had made a career out of the study of energy and how to apply it in practical ways (through massage therapy, yoga, and as a teacher), but it wasn't until Human Design found me that things clicked into place. Now, I teach other women entrepreneurs to leverage their energetic gifts to maximize profits and find happiness and ease in business.

Can we make a deal? Can you treat this book as a choose your own adventure novel? If I can teach one thing, make decisions aligned to your energy. TRUST YOURSELF IN THIS PROCESS. Not everything that works for others will be the right fit for you, and especially in business, you have to follow your path. Your passion and purpose will show you the way to prosperity much quicker than a 10 step process. You might come across something that isn't right in this moment or concepts and strategies that need to be modified to work for you. I intend to initiate your process, not give you a list of directives.

If it doesn't resonate for you, it's OK to let it go and move on to something that does. You know what is best for you, and I'm no one's guru. In fact, learning your Strategy and Authority (the basic tools of human design) will teach you how to be your own guru.

Working With Your Energy

I'm not sure where I heard this, but I want to give the author energetic credit: Strategy is how the universe communicates with you, and Authority is how you communicate with the universe. It doesn't get much simpler than that! And, if you can consistently use these 2 elements of your design, you won't need the fancy, complicated things in Human Design. Of course, in the rest of this book, I give you a taste of the fancy, complicated shit, but leveraging your energy will always come down to the things that have the most leverage and momentum: Strategy and Authority. .

My suggestion in approaching this book is to read this section first. Some things apply to every energy type. Even if this isn't the first time you've read about Strategy and Authority, it's a good review, and you may need it to understand the more specific information in your section. I might have some slightly different views than other teachers. This book is four books in one. Each energy type has its own section where you get the perspective from just your type. I talk about the Authority from the vantage of each type, plus how to set goals, business models, advertising and money.

If you read the other sections (which I recommend), you will notice some repetition. The same advice can work for all energy types, but how you approach it and position it is different.

Once you have read the portions of this book that apply to you, I suggest you go back and read the others as well. There may be gems in there that resonate with you more. Any strategy, model, or business can work for any energy type.

There is no "energy" that is better, more prosperous, or more successful in business than any other. So, keep trying until your Strategy and Authority light up.

INTRODUCTION

Let's Get Started!

If you are brand new to Human Design, you will need to get your chart or body graph. Many places online offer free charts, but one of my favorites is www.mybodygraph.com. When I first came to Human Design, I was curious but skeptical. I was in the camp of reading my horoscope on January 1 for fun but not putting any weight or thought behind it. Human Design combines and expands on concepts of Astrology, Chakras, Quantum Physics, the Kabbala, and the I Ching. While none were new to me, they aren't exactly mainstream science. We in the western world are conditioned to think of science as the holy grail of truth. So, if you're struggling like I was, try to suspend judgment until you've dug into working with **Strategy** and **Authority** for a few weeks.

In what feels like another lifetime, I used t teach Anatomy and Physiology. I've always been fascinated by the human body and spent over a decade as a massage therapist. I found that there is more to the story than science explains. There is an energy or aura that surrounds people. It is a fact. It may be anecdotal, but it is true nonetheless. Being in people's auras all the time made me curious. I couldn't deny that energy existed, but all the energy healing courses I took didn't satisfy my mind with how they explained the science behind their methods. But they worked. And some of them have been working for thousands of years. So what if I don't quite agree with their claim to "science?" Maybe we just don't have the tools to measure and explain it yet.

Besides, it doesn't matter what we believe. Everyone is an energetic, emotional, physical, and spiritual being. You can't just opt out because you don't believe it. Energy is operating behind the scenes, influencing your behavior and how you are best positioned to thrive in the world. If you want to use your natural energy consciously, Human Design is the most comprehensive explanation of the energetic dynamics at play that I have ever experienced. And, I've tried a lot.

Human Design is the closest thing I've found to Spiritual Anatomy.

It is a roadmap for your individualized energy and a method to use and leverage it so you can live your passion, purpose, and prosperity. So, here's the skinny on how Human Design explains how it works. Your soul has a purpose and a curriculum for the lessons and gifts you bring into the physical realm. It picks the time of your birth that has the optimal energetic environment to experience what you need in this lifetime.

Or, maybe it's random, and the purpose of life is that you just have to learn how to deal with your energy and optimize it, but I prefer to think that my soul chose this path. The neutrino stream determines the energetic environment, which is the particles traveling through space from the stars and planets that collide with your physical body and leave an energetic imprint. When you first enter the world, the neutrinos set the energetic tone you experience through life. When you're born, your energy is born. The neutrino stream is constantly changing and shifting. As you go through life, you are affected by it and other people's energy, but your baseline energy is determined at birth.

From here on, it will be helpful if you have your body graph handy so you have a visual reference. Depending on what the neutrinos are activating, it will affect your **Definition** in your chart (the colored in sections.) The definition will show you how energy moves in your body and establish a **Strategy** and **Authority** that will be your best response to your environment and a method for making decisions that will align with your energetic patterns. To make sense of your chart, you will need to understand all the shapes, numbers, symbols, and lines mean, so let's do a quick Anatomy lesson on the body graph.

Human Design Terms on the Body Graph

Design ← → Personality

Center
There are 9 energy centers. If a center is connected by a channel, it will be defined. Depending on the definition in your centers, it will determine your energy type and authority

Gate
There are 64 possible gates. The active gates in your chart are represented in 2 places. As the numbers in the centers on the body graph, and in the columns on the sides

Channel
When 2 gates meet, they form a Channel. When a channel is defined, the 2 centers that it connects will also be defined.

Unconscious/Design
The gates represented in this column are your unconscious energy. They are a snapshot of the energetic environment approximately 88 days before birth

Conscious/Personality
The gates represented in this column are your conscious energy. They are a snapshot of the energetic environment at birth

Planetary Symbol
The planet, represented by the symbol, is a modifier of how that gate is going to express in your life. Each planet has a different them, as does each gate.

Line
The line number is a further modifyer to your energy and how that gate is expressed. It is represented after the decimal point

The shapes (triangles and squares) are called **Centers**. On your chart, some will be colored in (**defined**) and some not (**undefined**.) If you are a **Reflector**, you have no **defined center**s in the body graph.

Depending on which **center** has definition, will determine your **Energy Type and Authority**. This is important because it is the foundational principle you use to influence and engage with your energy and use it intentionally.

On the **centers**, there are numbers; these correlate to the **Gates.** Again, some are shaded, and some are not. Each **gate** corresponds to a specific expression of energy. If two **gates** meet, they form a **Channel** that connects two **centers**. When you look at your chart, you will notice two columns with symbols, usually depicted in red on the left and black on the right. The left side is the neutrino stream 88 days before birth, which controls your **unconscious energy** (also called **design.**) The right side is a snapshot of the neutrino stream at the time of birth and determines your **conscious energy** (also called **personality.**)

Depending on what **planetary energy** they correlate to (the symbols) and the **activated gate** (the number), it will determine the context that energy influences. For example, the **gate** in your conscious sun (top right column) is the most potent energy in your chart and has a lot to do with how you show up in the world and interact with others.

The final piece I haven't mentioned yet is the number after the decimal point, this is called the **line**, and it further modifies the expression of the **gate**'s energy. The most critical line numbers are the ones in your sun/earth energy. These create your **Profile,** and give you insight into significant life themes, how you approach the world, and how others perceive your energy.

If you don't know the time of your birth, typically, the line numbers are what change the most throughout the day. If your birth certificate doesn't show the time of birth, the hospital you were born in might have a record of it, but if for whatever reason you can't find the birth time, your Profile is your next best clue. If I have someone who doesn't know when they were born, I will plug in different times to see what changes. If the Profile changes at some point, I will zero in on it to create a "best guess" at the time of birth.

My dad doesn't know what time he was born, and my grandma has long passed, taking that information with her. At about 8 PM on the day he was born, the profile shifts from a 2:4 to a 3:5. Making me think he was born late in the day because he is a classic 3:5, and I can't see much of the 2:4 in him. The moon is another fast-moving energy that shifts the gate activated fairly quickly. In my dad's case, the moon energy changes from gate 5 to gate 26 on the conscious and from 18-48 on the unconscious side. The effect was to create a channel between the Spleen and Will center and deactivate a channel between the Spleen and Root. So, a lot changed for him during the day he was born, which is a shame I don't know his actual birth time.

The Mechanics of Human Design

Now, let's talk about physiology; How things work! Everyone who teaches Human Design will filter it through their own experience and energy and present it differently, which is amazing! But, it can create some inconsistencies in the information you hear about Human Design. That means I'm bringing all my formal and informal learning and experience to Human Design, which includes intensive study of the human body and energetic healing, adult education, coaching, quantum physics, and a couple of decades of entrepreneurship, and that's just scratching the surface. The spin I put on Human Design will differ from someone else with a different background.

While I'm not claiming to be any more correct than anyone else who teaches Human Design, I want you to understand the mechanics of how energy flows in the body so that when you come across conflicting information, you can decide what you want to believe. One of my pet peeves is that **Manifesting Generators** are a hybrid. It makes no sense if you look at the way the energy of an MG works. I digress.

Human Design offers a method for making decisions that align with your spiritual expression. It's a method for determining what is true for *you*. Consider Human Design an experiment where you try experiences on for size to see if they are right for you and glean your truth. If you come across something that doesn't seem right, trust your inner knowing and let the rest flow through you. Don't waste your time and energy on things that aren't a fit for you, but you also want to be aware of when you're creating resistance and mental drama. You don't have to explain (to me, others, or yourself!). You do you boo, and let the rest slide on by.

Everything in this book is meant to suggest something to try and figure out if it works for you. It's not a directive, which is why I will often use the passive voice, or words like maybe and other wimpy literary vices. While it may take the punch out of my writing, the goal is to create your meaning and methods of operating in life and business. I'm not your guru; Human Design is not your guru. It's meant to be a path towards being your own guru, and that is the most beautiful outcome I can imagine.

Every human being operating in their sovereignty and power.
Now that gives me all the good tingles.

I want to take a slight detour into quantum energy theory for a moment. I love Human Design because it gives you a method to align your vibration with the things you want to manifest. But, there is one thing that always bothered me post "The Secret." It made out that it was all about thought. That thoughts create things, and all you have to do is hold positive thoughts, and you go from driving a pretend car in your chair to the real thing.

There are two problems I see with this. The first is that the human mind is not programmed to think positive thoughts 100% of the time. It is part of our survival programming to have a bias towards negative thoughts, so if you're 50/50 positive to negative thoughts, you're doing great, so stop beating yourself up over "negative" thoughts.

The second problem is that thought energy is not creative until it becomes words and actions. You can think all day about a car, but unless you go out and do something, it's not going to manifest. Thoughts assign meaning to situations (that are actually neutral until thought makes it mean something.) Thoughts create emotions, and emotions drive you to act and speak. And it's those actions and words that the universe matches in frequency to bring you situations of the same vibration.

It's not thoughts we need to police, although you need to create awareness around them and the emotions they feed. It's not even emotions, although understanding how you react to and what triggers emotions is critical. What we need to manage are **actions and words**. Human Design gives you a way of acting on things aligned to your highest frequency through **Strategy and Authority.**

Human Design is the science of differentiation. Each human is uniquely different. Even two people with the same energetic baseline (twins, for example) will have different conditioning agents (Experiences, relationships, situations, personality, thought processes, beliefs, etc.) that will cause their energy to be uniquely their own. **Conditioning** happens throughout life, but a lot of conditioning will occur in the first seven years. Before the age of 7, the brain hasn't developed critical thinking enough to assess what people say is true or not, and it's a survival directive to learn how to become part of the tribe. So, when a child hears something from parents, siblings, teachers, etc., like "People with money are bad," It becomes part of their belief system about money.

These beliefs form the unconscious operating system. Unless you have reason to question your beliefs at some point in your life, they often end up running the show for people in areas like self-worth, money, success, relationships, talents, etc. Even after age 7, most people don't have reason to question their beliefs, so you can find that un-resourceful belief systems follow you into adulthood.

For most people, it takes a trauma to start the process of bringing their beliefs to light, questioning if they serve, and reprogramming with more resourceful beliefs. Chipping away at past conditioning and being aware of how we pick up conditioning in the present is essential for success. I recommend a daily practice of awareness to address the conditioning you pick up. But I'm getting ahead of myself.

Regardless, you can't avoid conditioning, but you can control what you make it mean. Where you are open is where you go to the school of life. You get to experience that energy in all the different ways, and it is not always available to you. As a spiritual entrepreneur, you sell from your openness.

Your openness is where you have the opportunity to learn and grow. It is where you can hold space for others to process their energy and empathize with it. In the Human Design world, it's easy to fall into thinking definition=good and openness=bad. It's not the case at all! It is just a different way of experiencing energy. Your openness is where you have superpowers.

Let's take the **Solar Plexus center** or the **Emotional center**. Approximately 50% of people have it defined. These people have a pattern to the way they experience emotion. They have a specific experience called the emotional wave. There are different types of emotional waves, but they generally have emotional energy that is consistently available to them, and it is their own experience of it.

If it is defined, this is your **Authority**. Your way of making aligned decisions is to ride out your emotions in a situation, then do what you feel is correct when you have emotional clarity. For the other half of the world, you get to experience all the emotions, just not all the time. You will act as a mirror that amplifies energy where you have openness.

In short, this empathy means that sometimes you are experiencing your own emotions, and sometimes you pick up on someone else's energy and magnify it. As a child, I often heard that I was emotional. I always had big emotions and lots of them. Now, I realize that many of the feelings I experienced were not my own. I amplified people's emotional energy and didn't realize it or know how to handle it.

It wasn't until Human Design found me that I recognized this mechanism. I've always had people in my inner circle with defined emotional centers, so I never really questioned whether the emotions I experienced were mine. I just assumed they were and rode everyone else's wave. Now, with awareness, I can ask myself if I need to spend the emotional energy on something or if it's someone else's. When I'm being extra magnifying, I can remove myself from others' energy and find my emotional baseline before re-engaging with the world.

Typically, where you do not have definition is where you can pick up conditioning. In the **centers**, we call this the **not-self theme.** Because you can pick up on external energy, your openness is where you can pick up ideas, beliefs, and ways of being that are not true to you and your energy. This is conditioning at its core. If you have definition in an area (**center, gate, channel**), you will experience that energy in a particular way, and it will be consistent and predictable.

Many of your strengths and abilities will come from your definition. It is your unique expression of that energy, and it is consistent throughout your life. You can express your energy in healthy, higher vibration states or lower frequency, or shadow states even with definition. The key to both conditioning and operating at a high frequency in your definition is awareness, conscious action, and aligning your decisions to your **Strategy** and **Authority**.

It's essential to understand the mechanics of how energy flows in the body to utilize yours best. Energy enters the body through the head and root centers. I'm not talking about the energy you get from food that your mitochondria use to fuel the body's physical functions. I'm talking about quantum energy, source energy, spiritual energy, whatever you call that animating energy that gives us life, purpose, and passion. This energy is trying to find the path of least resistance to the throat center where it is expressed and takes form as a manifestation. The form this manifestation takes will depend on the vibration or frequency of the energy you put out as you react and respond to the situations and environment with actions and words. You seek to use the concepts and methods of Human Design to make decisions that align to your highest frequency expression of energy.

The Head and Root centers are called **pressure centers**. Right away, your brain will try to assign meaning to this, but all it means is that energy in these centers creates a need to respond to it in some way to move the energy. If you create resistance and interference to the energy (through your thoughts, feelings, and actions), it will amplify the uncomfortable sensation known as "stress."

One way to think about this is that anything that you become aware of is a stimulus that your **Strategy** and **Authority** will guide you to respond to. You do this to create awareness around how you respond and react (in Human Design, we call this a conditioned response) and learn the guidance system of your **Authority**.

Next, we have the **awareness centers**: Anja for awareness of mental and conceptual energy, Spleen for awareness of physical, instinctual, intuitive energy, and the Solar Plexus to understand emotional energy. Definition in these centers will mean you have a consistent way of processing this energy. Where you are defined, you won't pick up the influence of others. Undefined or open will mean you have an unreliable energy source in that area but experience a wider variety in your experience of it, and you can pick up others' energy in these areas.

Motor centers, when defined, will give you a reliable source of power to move energy towards the throat. The sacral center, for example, generates life force energy, giving those with definition a consistent source of energy to create, do and build. If this is defined, you are a **Generator**, or a **Manifesting Generator**, which is a sub-type of **Generator**, so same-same in this case.

This is why **Generator**s are called "The Builders." Their sacral motor gives them the energy to take on and complete projects. The sacral motor is always on. If a **Generator** doesn't have the energy for something, it means it is not an aligned action for them, or they are misusing their sacral energy doing things they don't like doing that drains their will to live err... life force energy. If you're a **Projector**, **Manifestor**, or **Reflector** thinking, wait a minute, I can do things too! Oh yes, you can! You just use a different mechanism in your energy to do, create and complete.

The other three **motor center**s operate in a pulse, so it is either on or off, but it is still consistent. The Solar Plexus center as a motor will move the energy in an emotional wave, and depending on which **channel** is activated, it will affect your experience of that energy. The root center will have a steady, slow rhythm, and the Will (also called the heart or ego) center will stay on until it needs rest, have a period of recovery then come back online.

You can still accomplish things in life and business if you don't have any motors defined (some **Projector**s and **Reflector**s). Still, you will need to be discerning in what you apply your energy towards. Your energy will be affected by the energetic environment created by the transiting planets and neutrino stream and the people in your immediate environment. What this might look like in your business is outsourcing some repetitive work and saving your energy for creating and serving customers when it is on.

That leaves two centers that we don't usually define by their type. The throat center is how we express and sets the frequency of what we put out into the world. The G-center has to do with identity and direction.

It doesn't matter whether your centers are defined or not; this is how energy flows. Depending on whether your head, root, and/or throat centers are defined, you will process it differently. And depending on what definition you have along the way, the conditioning around a situation, plus the energetic environment of the neutrino stream, will affect how you influence the vibration of the energy that passes through you.

You can either be intentional about the way you manage your thoughts, emotions and energy or allow it to run on the default settings of how you are conditioned to think, feel and react. I aim to give you a field guide on using your energy intentionally. But, it isn't for the faint of heart. What it takes is radical responsibility for yourself. I say radical because it is uncommon to find someone who has decided to ignore all the conditioning, socialization, and the culture of choosing to think we are at the effect of the environment, people, and situations in our life. While you don't have control over many things, situations, or people's actions and words, you do have control over:

- What you make it mean (This will set the tone of your emotions and regulate your reactions and emotional response to your environment)
- How you speak and act in response (This is how you send out a frequency for the universe to match and bring you more of that vibration)
- Your awareness of your past conditioning and how it influences your thoughts, feelings, and actions (This is how you create results on purpose rather than operating from your unconscious, ego-self)

Does this mean that you will never fall into a victim mindset again? No.

But you strengthen your awareness of it and can move out of it towards a more empowering state. A state where you can regulate your emotions, take intentional action, and take over the world. Wahahahahaha. Most people have the conditioning to think in terms of all or nothing, success or fail, yes or no, black or white. You will want to see your journey through life and business as an experiment. Sometimes you take aligned action, and it takes you to the things you want, and sometimes that same aligned action will bring you to a lesson, growth, or confrontation. If you make it mean that you failed or made a mistake, you're missing the point, and the universe will continue to repeat that lesson until you get what you need from it.

So, do me a favor and set the intention to be open to the experiences meant for you. Stop judging yourself, and become the observer of your thoughts, feelings, and actions. Human Design is best approached with lightness.

Release the need to make it produce results immediately. It will work fast, but you will slow your progress if you create resistance by forcing your energy. Drop the gravity and have some fun with the experiment. Learn what makes your energy the most awesome tool for your life and in service of your customers. You, yes, you have something unique and special to bring to the world, and if you get out of your own way, you can get on with it.

So, if you haven't already, grab your body graph and find your Energy Type and Authority.

STRATEGY AND AUTHORITY
ALL TYPES

STRATEGY AND AUTHORITY If you apply one thing from Human Design, learn how to use your **Strategy** and **Authority**. It is the foundation for leveraging your energy and does all the heavy lifting in aligning to your highest potential. There are many layers to the Human Design System, but the simplest and most profound results will come from learning and living your **Strategy** and **Authority**. It is easy to get distracted by details about gates, lines, etc. If things have gone a little sideways in life and business, chances are you've drifted from your **Strategy** and **Authority**.

It's not that all the other things aren't necessary, but if you aren't using **Strategy** and **Authority**, it's like trying to navigate the death star with a paperclip. **Strategy** and **Authority** get you in the vicinity of your goals and desires, and the rest will take care of those one-degree shifts to fine-tune your path. Usually, they do it naturally without the effort on your part. If you're not using **Strategy** and **Authority**, nothing else really matters. When you align yourself with all the good things in life meant for you, your energy naturally expresses itself through your gifts.

So, while it may be basic, it is the most powerful way to leverage your power and get to your goals and desires fastest.

Authority type depends on which center(s) you have defined. There is a hierarchy, so the first center defined on the list will be your authority. This is the order:

- Solar Plexus Center (Emotional Authority)
- Sacral Center (Sacral Authority)
- Splenic Center (Splenic Authority)
- Will Center (Ego Authority)
- Definition of a combination of Head, Anja, and Throat centers, with no other centers defined (Mental Projectors with Environmental Authority)
- No centers defined (Reflectors with Lunar Authority)

My recommendation for all energy types is to create a morning routine or ritual where you check-in and get to know and love your base-level energy. Set an intention to use your **Strategy** and **Authority** and bring awareness to your thoughts. Notice where you are picking up conditioning and operating from not-self each day, and as you go through your day, find time to pause and be aware of what you're thinking and feeling. If you're interested in creating your own energy routine, I have another book you should check out called "Finding your Business Mojo with Human Design."

Relevant to all energy types:

1. There is no energy type (or expression of energy) that is better or worse than any other at business (or anything!) Everyone has access to all energy of the bodygraph, but some energy will come more naturally and consistently to you. Just because you don't have a definition in a specific area doesn't mean that you can't do something or access the essence of that energy. Avoid conditioning yourself by feeding the not-self belief of "Just because I have/don't have means I can't do/be/have whatever. One I often hear is, "I don't have a defined motor center, so I can't work." Be aware of the stories you tell yourself about yourself and your energy. If you're going to assign meaning, make sure it is resourceful for you to do so.

2. Your desires are for you. If you want something, you have the energetic capacity to bring it into being. If it wasn't for you, your soul would not have the desire to do what it is you want to do. Business is about service, so at the core of your desire to be an entrepreneur, you want to serve others, help them solve a problem, and improve their life in some way. Money will follow service.

3. All energy types respond to the environment around them in their way. **Manifestors** need to be inspired by something to initiate their process. **Generators** (and MG's) respond directly to their environment through awareness. **Projectors** respond to recognition and invitation. **Reflectors** sample their environment and react to it over a 28-day lunar cycle.

4. Most people have the conditioning to listen to their minds and thoughts. Very few people question the truth of thought. We think that because we believe it, it must be true. One of my most profound learnings was that I get to choose what is true, and if I don't like a thought, I can choose to believe differently. What guides my truth now is my inner Authority. I find my truth by going within, not outside of myself, and it is the most wonderful shift you can learn to make. The role of the mind is to take in outer information, process it, and present it to the inner Authority

to respond to. The ego will often hijack the mind, create drama, and convince you to use your mind as your inner Authority. Once again, it comes down to practicing awareness of self, thoughts, and when you're pulled into making decisions from the not-self.

5. It will take practice to get good at listening to your Authority. It is essential to be intentional about bringing your **Strategy** and **Authority** into your daily life. It is easy to get distracted by all the information on your design, but if you drift away from the basic, core principle of Human Design, the fine details don't mean anything.

6. Using **Strategy** and **Authority** is a relatively simple process, but there are two major pitfalls to watch out for: Mind and Ego. They work together, and the main priority is to maintain survival and the status quo. Mind and ego don't like change. Even if it's a good change, they are probably used to being in charge since that's how most people operate. The mind serves the inner Authority by being an external Authority. It works to process information from the environment. You're using your external Authority right now to read, learn and process the stimulus of information, then the inner Authority takes over to determine yes or no, truth or not truth, for me or not for me. In short, your inner Authority drives, and your outer Authority provides the information you need to navigate. But, if not trained, the mind is one hell of a back seat driver. Actually, most of the time, it's the ego disguised as the mind in the driver's seat. Be aware when the mind is making things up for you to respond to. It is about making your mind your ally and noticing when it is trying to sway your decisions from your inner Authority.

7. Bringing awareness to the mind and the thoughts running the show is important. Journaling and freewriting are excellent ways to bring attention to the unconscious thoughts behind the scenes. This is also an essential part of learning how your conditioning may influence your actions.

8. Some energies have, let's say, challenging names. (eg. Gate of the

Fighter, Channel of Struggle) Alternatively, you may have some "positive" energy like "The Money Line" or Channel of Power. Don't let the names fool you! All energy in your chart is potential energy and will have a high and low-frequency expression (and everything in between.) You learn how to manage your energy and learn the lessons you are here (on earth) to learn through the shadow *and* the gift frequencies. The challenging energy in your chart is for you to grow and express yourself in the world—ditto for learning how to use your gifts. The gate of the fighter, for example, can do amazing work in social justice at a high frequency, as they can discern what is worth fighting for, but at a low frequency can attract a lot of unnecessary conflicts. Similarly, the money line at a low frequency can be miserly and hoard resources, limiting their flow. So, don't assign too much meaning to the energy in your chart. Contemplate it lightly, look for patterns of how it plays out, and follow your **Strategy** and **Authority** towards the experiences and expressions of your high-frequency energy.

9. Human Design is an experiment. No one will make aligned decisions all the time. Be kind to yourself! You can always re-set and start using **Strategy** and **Authority** again. Stop assigning the term failure to situations. Sometimes you can make an aligned decision, and it leads to something you didn't want. Your **Authority** can lead you to your desires, but sometimes it leads you to growth, lessons, and the experiences that develop your skills. I like to think of it this way: if I get a lesson, it means I'm preparing for something better than the thing I thought I wanted.

Now, go to the section on your energy type first. Read up on how your energy type applies the concepts of Strategy and Authority. Each type will also learn how their energy type does best with goals, business models, advertising, and money.

BOOK ONE

REFLECTORS

NO DEFINED CHANNELS OR CENTERS

Reflectors

| STRATEGY | NOT SELF THEME | SELF THEME |

Wait a Lunar Cycle (28 DAYS) — STRATEGY

Disappointment — NOT SELF THEME

Surprise Delight — SELF THEME

Are you tired of being told how rare a bird you are yet? I mean, one in every 100 people isn't that rare. It's not rare like your chances of winning the lottery. In a world of 8 billion people, 1% is a lot of people. 80 million actually. I hope the other types are reading this, realizing that Reflectors make up a huge market share, and start creating more content for Reflectors. It can be challenging even to find more than a footnote in much of the human design world about Reflectors.

Your pace is different from the rest of the world. In the beginning, I bet it is hard to swallow that you can't act on the big things until you have spent nearly a month ruminating on it. I also suspect that once you get in the groove of your lunar cycle, it will feel like coming home.

Can I give you permission to drop the conditioning and external pressure to move quickly? If you stop trying to match the energy and pace of every Generator that comes across your path, you will find the world much more peaceful, surprising and abundant.

For you, it really is about slowing down to speed up.

INTRODUCTION TO BEING A REFLECTOR

YOUR ROLE in a community is to sample energy and determine its health. What this looks like in human design terms is that your open centers soak up the energy around you. If something is off with the energy, you know. It is also very important to clear out not-self energy, and I recommend making it part of your routine to recognize and manage the energy you carry.

Consciously letting go of not-self energy will help you stay grounded and focused in your business. Most of the time, I recommend a morning routine to set intentions for the day and plan out your workload, but for Reflectors, an evening routine to shed excess stress and energy can also be helpful.

Overstimulation can be a thing for you. It will help to ensure that your environment feels good.

I typically don't mention much about the variables because they don't mean anything until you align with your energy. They are more of a fine-tuning application rather than something to focus on and live by. But… for you, the environment is critical to the point where you can't make progress until you have your environment sorted out. Being in a nourishing environment will help you manage your energy and maximize it. If you're over stimulated, your environment can help you get grounded so you can free up some energy to actually think about the things that will move the needle in life and business.

At the time of writing (late 2021) **www.geneticmatrix.com** has this info on their free chart, but you have to dig for it a bit. On the dropdown menu that defaults to quantum, select "Design." It is on the side as "Environment." Start playing around with setting your surroundings up in a way that nurtures you. If you work in one space, consider how you can recreate your environment to suit. I want to caution you that changing your environment still isn't a replacement for strategy and authority, so please don't rabbit hole this too deep. When making significant changes to your living environment (like moving), take a full 28 days to consider it.

Pressure and stress are going to be very challenging for you. Typically your response will be to shut down. Setting your business up to minimize pressure is critical. How and when you generate income, what structures you have for dealing with clients and conflict, and what to do when you don't have the energy to do something that needs to get done are just a few considerations for you.

A business model with multiple avenues of income, some passive, might be a better setup than two major launches a year. Consider how you can create diverse income streams so you don't have all your income coming from one place. Hiring help in your business will free you up to do what you do best. You are the bird's eye view of a situation, and your power is in evaluation. Doing grunt work is not a great use of your energy. If you aren't in a place to hire help yet, find when you are activated as a Generator or MG for the more mundane tasks.

Without definition in any center, it means you do not have consistent physical, mental or emotional energy of your own. You're going to pick it up from the energetic environment caused by the neutrinos from the transits and the energy of people in your aura. The energy of people around you won't make as much of an impact as the transits and moon. Your aura will naturally deflect others' energy. One of the things you have going for you is that you seem to know when energy isn't yours. Because most energy isn't, you don't have this confusion that other energy types do about the mechanic of empathetically absorbing others' energy and amplifying it.

Until I met human design, I didn't realize that my undefined emotional center soaked up all those intense emotions from everyone around me. I just assumed they were mine. It never occurred to me that I could opt-out. Reflectors naturally seem to sense that not everything you experience (thoughts, emotions, or physical energy) is yours.

I should clarify that once you react to one of these drive-by emotions or energy, it is your experience. It can be misleading to label it as "not mine." The energy of the other will initiate you, and you will experience that energy (emotional, physical, or mental) through their definition as if you were defined in that way. Once you react to the "other" energy, it is yours. Your emotions but experienced through the other's wave. Your thoughts and sensations but experienced through the other's definition. I live with a defined solar plexus. If he comes home in a bad mood, it's still on me to be aware of the mechanic and choose not to react and amplify that energy.

. . .

Recognizing and managing when you're reactive to others' emotions is a ninja skill for Reflectors.

Your openness is a mirror to the people around you. Unlike the Manifestors (who also have a repelling aura), you are more likely to blend into a community and not be noticed than stir people up. This can be a bit challenging since you don't want to be invisible as an entrepreneur. Your aura is going to be difficult for people to read. You come off as quite mysterious to the rest of the world. Historically, Reflectors have been the mystics, medicine women, and magic workers of the world.

Others will probably make assumptions about you depending on how they see themselves. This gives you a lot of insight into your customer's fears, desires, and needs. After you engage with a customer, it might be worthwhile to reflect on what you absorbed from your meeting for a few moments. Are there any insights into your ideal customer that you can add to your marketing and messaging? Is there anything you need to let go of before getting on with your day? You might also find it helpful to have some form of ritual or meditation before going into meetings with clients to set your intentions and energetic boundaries.

I have a question for you. How did Projectors get the moniker of "ultimate guide?" I feel like Reflectors missed the boat on claiming that title. Sure, sure, Projectors help guide the energy of others, but with all your open space, you allow others to see into their soul. Not really, but it sounded good. Open centers are where you go to the school of life. They are where you get to experience the whole range of energy. If you have definition, you experience that energy in one way, your way. But, Reflectors can help others process and see their energy to learn and grow. Your ability to appraise how healthy energy is makes you an amazing coach, guide, or teacher. You are good at evaluating the energy of a person, place, or situation. If you are acting as a guide, you can ask the right questions for the other to figure out their process.

Strategy: To wait a 28 day lunar cycle

When you learn about your design and find out you have to wait 28 days to make decisions, I bet you were like F That! No one likes to wait. I suspect you've spent a lifetime being encouraged to move faster than your instinct. So when you surrender to the rhythm in your body, energy, and life, it can surprise you how much easier things start to come to you. That is how it works too. As you relax into your flow, life brings you all the resources, clients, relationships, and opportunities you need.

You don't really have a separate strategy and authority. What initiates your process is much the same as a Generator. Something will present itself for you to respond to it, and because your energy works on a 28-day cycle, you need to feel the decision out through all the phases of your energetic cycle. You might think that your energy is all random all the time, influenced by stars, planets, and people. But, the strongest influence is going to be the moon. As its energy affects the earth's energy, it will engage with your energy. You have definition in your chart in the gates. As the moon moves through its cycle, it will activate different channels and centers for you. These activations will be predictable. The moon is in each gate for approximately 10 hours.

The energy of the moon in the natal chart relates to your motivations. Without understanding the mechanism of your moon energy, you can feel out of place in the world, off-center, and struggle with not understanding why you do the things you do. Every energy type experiences the transient energy of the moon, but for you, it is what creates consistency in your energy. When you are thinking about your energy in terms of leveraging it, the snapshot of the day you were born doesn't tell the whole story. You need 28 days to tell the story of the moon and how it dances through activations of gates, channels, and centers with your existing energy. That is what creates your baseline energy.

Other energy types aren't as sensitive to the energy of the moon. My theory is because they have energy that is always consistently available to them, that grounds them in the energy of their body and the world, they don't notice the transiting energy as much because it is subtle compared to their baseline energy. Take a look at the gates in your earth for clues on what will help you feel grounded and balanced.

GeneneticMatrix.com has a service where you can compare the moon cycle to your chart, and it will summarize the activations for you. It is part of their paid services, but once you have your moon activations and correlate them to the day of the moon cycle rather than the day of the month, you can re-use the information unless you move to a different time zone. You can also McGuyver it and go through the chart generator, putting in other times to find when it changes, then note it. This would be a tedious way to save a few dollars, but you might find it interesting to do it this way to get very familiar with your chart and how it engages with the moon's energy and other activations.

As the moon moves through all the gates, one of 3 scenarios will occur:

1. It activates a gate that does not have existing definition for you, and you do not have an existing activation from your own chart that completes a channel. In this case, you will experience the gate energy, while the moon activates that gate.

2. It activates a gate that you already have defined in your chart. You will experience an enhanced energy of that gate while the moon does it's thing there.

3. It activates a gate that meets one of your existing gates, completing a channel. This will create "definition" in centers and channels for the time the moon is in that activation.

You have an extended processing time because your energy changes from day to day, moment to moment, as the moon moves through the gates. You need time to figure out what it all means and what is self-energy vs. not-self energy. The question for Reflectors is to ask, "Who am I *today?*" and feel out what is right for you in this iteration of you. Some of the transient energy can be very powerful, and the waiting period will help you determine whether it is a good thing long-term or whether that energy will move on.

Because the lunar cycle and how it engages with your energy is consistent over 28 days, you can use it to plan your business. If you know you need to complete something, you might find when your sacral center is activated, you will have the energy to work like a Generator. Maybe a day where you batch your social media content? Or, consider scheduling consultations on days when the gate of provocation is activated. Feeling out your cycle for the patterns and consistencies in your energy will help you maximize the beautiful variation that makes you unique.

Like the mental Projectors, you don't have any consistent physical or body energy. Finding practices to help you be present with your physical body will be an important part of your physical and mental health. Things that help you stay grounded and present are going to be valuable. Undefined Head and Anja will want to occupy your mind with thinking about things that don't matter and will often try to distract you with over-identification with the past or future. A daily practice to interrupt the mind chatter and observe what you think will help you. (Typically, we call this meditation) but it can take on many forms, and not all practices and rituals will appeal to you all the time, so giving yourself some variety in your awareness practice can help you stick with it.

Tracking transits is a valuable tool. It will help you sort out what energy is passing by at that moment, and you can also use it to plan in your business. The moon energy is not the only planetary energy at play. It may seem overwhelming at first to track all 13 planetary energies. So my recommendation is to get comfortable with tracking the moon, then add in the sun gate. It is the next most influential energy, and it changes every 4ish days.

Then, I would add in the nodes simply because they are easy to track because they move very slowly. The rest, I would check when you do your energy routine in the morning. GeneticMatrix.com has a daily Neutrino Conditioning Weather Report on their home screen that shows that day's transits, and I would approach it by looking for any key activations that energy creates for you.

The north and south node energy move very slowly. They are activated for 4ish months, and the nodes influence the environment and how we perceive the past and future. Right now (late 2021), the north and south nodes create a channel between gate 20 of the throat and gate 34 in the sacrum. This means that every person in the world has the energetic capacity to be a Manifesting Generator (and every child born in this timeframe is a Manifesting Generator.) Because it is slow energy, it's relatively easy to be aware of the node energy and how it affects you.

Signature: Surprise Not-self theme: Disappointment

Your signature is how you know you are on the right path. When you feel surprised, you are following your strategy and making decisions from your authority. This is a good health check for your energy. If you are experiencing more disappointment than surprise, you want to look at how you are making decisions and where you might be operating from conditioning and/or not-self.

In true Reflector form, surprise can be a little illusive. I mean, WTF is surprise anyway? I guess that it's an emotion that has never really crossed your mind before you knew about your Human Design type. What does the sensation of surprise feel like in your body? For me, it is lifting and spreading across my chest, and animation and energy in my face (my eyebrow raises when I'm surprised.) Your version may differ, but I want you to know the physical feeling of surprise.

Now that you know what to look for start to note when you feel surprised. You will probably find that you feel your signature more often than you think. If you find surprise challenging to pin down, try borrowing the Manifestor signature of peace. Now, my beautiful cynic, what would/does surprise you in your business? Is it ease? A big paycheck? What about attracting amazing people to work with?

I call you a cynic because of your not-self theme of disappointment. You need to track and notice the ways the world is a beautiful, amazing, and surprising place, or you start finding more and more evidence that the world is disappointing. What you notice you get more of, so I want you to be careful what you put your energy towards. Feed the surprise, let go of the disappointment. Manage this part of your energy, and much of the rest falls into place.

AUTHORITY FOR REFLECTORS

AUTHORITY IS DETERMINED BY THE CENTER(S) YOU HAVE
DEFINED

AUTHORITY FOR REFLECTORS

LUNAR AUTHORITY (1% of the population)

I first want to point out that you only use your full authority for moderate to major life decisions and not the minor everyday choices that are just part of life. I mean, you could die waiting 28 days to make some decisions, so when it is not a major thing you're deciding on, you go with what your body feels like at that moment, which means getting into your physical body in the present moment to make a decision. For these low-level decisions, I recommend that you read the mental Projector authority section for some actionable advice on your day-to-day decisions.

There will be a 28-day rhythm and pattern to your energy and emotions. Awareness of your patterns will be key to aligning to your energetic gifts. One thing that many Reflectors find valuable is to track a few moon cycles with a journal. (Actually, I recommend always keeping a moon journal. This way, you can go back and find patterns that will help you operate best with your energy.) It is also valuable to know your typical state at the new moon, for example, that way, you know what your usual energy is at that stage, and it can help you make aligned energetic decisions about things medium and small in the moment. For example, you might know that around the new moon, you get a surge of emotional energy, which can influence emotional decisions at that time. Or, around the waxing moon, you seem to have higher willpower energy, so you might make commitments that need that type of energy then.

When making decisions that aren't small but still not big is that by the time you need to make the decision, it usually isn't the first time it's come across your awareness. You may have been considering something and feeling it out for a cycle already and just weren't conscious of it. Take hiring a business coach, for example. If you're reading this book, you are at least aware of and or curious about human design and entrepreneurship and want to learn how to improve your business. If you've been on the internet in the last several years, you're probably aware that business coaching is an option. So, if an opportunity came up to join a coaching program (mine perhaps?) and cart closed in 2 weeks, you would probably have enough information to make an aligned decision for yourself within that timeframe of whether it was a yes or no.

Let's talk about what constitutes a "big" thing for you for a minute. There are essentially two things that will rock your world the most:

1. Who you spend your time with: Who you live with and who you work with

2. The environment you spend most of your time in: Where you live/work

Decisions about roommates, spouses, living and working environment, and colleagues/bosses are always worth an entire 28-day cycle. At least. I realize that you won't have the luxury of that much time, especially with something like a job, but if you take a position, consider it on probation for 28 days and have a backup/escape plan if it doesn't work out. If a person or environment isn't right, GET OUT!

As an entrepreneur, major shifts in your business model or product, messaging and marketing plan, significant investments, and long-term business partners/associates will also need 28 days of consideration. I would go so far as to say clients as well, but that's probably not feasible, so go with the method for making small and medium decisions with them and have an escape clause built in after 28 days.

I'm going to describe the typical energy of the moon at each of its phases. I say "typical" because you, my dear, are far from typical. Your own energy plus the shifting energy of the transits and people around you and your menstrual cycle will also influence how you experience this energy. There will be a subtly to understanding all the layers of your energetic makeup that takes time to sort out. That's why you journal: to find the patterns in your expression of energy.

Certain phases of the menstrual cycle will carry similar energy to phases of the moon, so I'm marking the moon cycle along with the menstrual phase. Usually, but not always your cycle will naturally align itself to the new or full moon.

1.   The New Moon

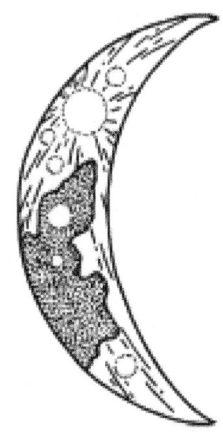

| *Moon is at its Smallest*

Menstruation/bleeding phase: cycle day 1-7ish

Archetype: Wise woman/crone

Energy: Yin, feminine, passive

- This is a good time to reset and prepare for a new phase. Rest, reflect and plan are good things to focus on.
- It is a time to clean house emotionally, physically, spiritually, and energetically. If it isn't working for you, let it go. It's OK to shed what no longer serves you.
- This is a time in your cycle that you are at your most powerful in a psychic sense. You will find that this is an excellent time to assess the previous cycle and make plans for the new one to come. You will want to use this time to reflect, journal, and connect with your intuitive and mystic superpowers.
- Historically, women retreated from society during menstruation,

sometimes choosing to menstruate together to amplify the psychic energy of this time

- Your energy may be at a lower ebb than other times in your cycle. It's OK to rest or take on more passive activities.
- As the beginning of a new cycle, it is the time to plant seeds, literally or figuratively, and can be a good time to start a new project or endeavor
- In your business, it's time to receive inspiration, dream, and plan. It might be a great week to outline your idea for a program or create a launch plan. It is less ideal to launch a program or carry out a program this week.
- If possible, try to plan downtime in your life and business for these weeks.

2. Waxing Moon

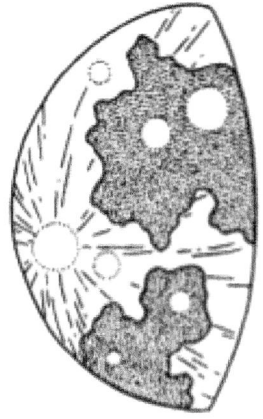

| *Moon is Growing*

Pre-ovulation/follicular phase: cycle day (end of bleed) 4-7ish to Ovulation (approx cycle day 14)

Archetype: Maiden

Energy: Yang, masculine, active, summer

- You are at your creative maximum during this time and will be able to take ideas and make them a reality.
- Now is a great time to get things done. You will experience more energy to build and accomplish something.
- It's a great time to build that program or product and drive forward with your business and life.
- Get moving! Move the physical body, or shake up your environment if you feel so inclined.
- Reflectors can be sensitive to their environment, but at this phase, you are more resilient than normal, so explore, play, create, experiment, and experience new things

3. **Full Moon**

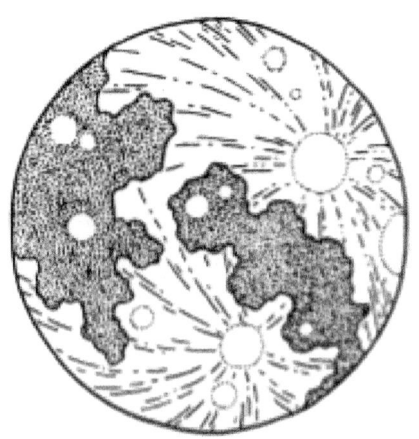

| *Moon is at its Largest*

Ovulation phase cycle day 14-21 (ish)

Archetype: Mother

Energy: Yin, feminine, passive

- You may experience heightened emotion during this time as this is when the moon's influence is at its fullest, and the moon is the planet of emotions.
- This may not be a great time for significant changes or decisions as you may be inclined to make emotional decisions
- Connect with your heart energy, and desires. Are you headed towards what you really want, or is an adjustment needed to course correct? It is a good time to illuminate and reflect on what is working and what isn't
- You may want to focus on nurturing yourself at this time. Take a bubble bath or a nap. Or both! Get enough sleep—Mother yourself how you always wanted to be mothered.
- It can be a good time to do shadow or inner child work as you will have a greater capacity for compassion for yourself.
- This is a time to reap the rewards, and for some, it is hard to allow yourself to receive. Energetically, receiving is just as important as giving, so if you have trouble allowing money to flow in, now is a good time to clear that out.

4. **Waning Moon**

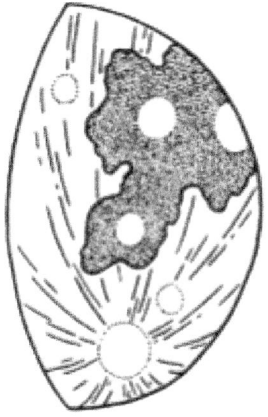

Moon is Getting Smaller

29

Pre Menstrual cycle day 21-start of bleed

Archetype: Medicine Woman

Energy: Yang, masculine, active

- This is a time of completion and preparation for the new cycle. You will want to close energetic loops from this cycle.
- There is unusual energy at this time, like the space between. You will have the urge to wrap things up and be looking ahead, and it can seem like a fallow time, but you are busy making preparations.
- Next week, you want to clear space to have downtime during the new moon/menstruation.
- In your business, this is a good time to deliver on what you have promised to your customers and can be a benificial time to run your programs, or even a good time to close cart on something that has had a longer runway or lead up.
- Take time to breathe and reflect. Are you doing the things that align with your energy? Is your business serving you? Do you love what you are doing? Is there an opportunity to change something so it will serve better? Are you ignoring yourself or something critical? What does your business need from you, and what do you need from your business?

The other thing that goes hand in hand with your authority of tracking your moon cycle is to follow the transits. I have an excellent freebie to help you track both your moon cycle and transits at **www.carmenfarrellknapp. com/journal**. One thing about your aura is that it will naturally repel the energy of others to some degree. (If you live with someone or spend hours a day with them, you won't be immune to their energy.) In general, the energetic environment created by the transits will affect you the more than being around others casually.

The easiest way to compare how your energy engages with planetary energy is to print your chart and laminate it. This will give you something to use dry erase markers to show the temporary energy overlaid on your permanent energy. (You can also draw in the energy of people to see how their energy engages with yours if you know their birth date.) Then you look for patterns in your chart that complete channels and activate centers for you.

You will need a source of information on the transits. There are blogs and podcasts that will show the transits of that day, but it is more challenging to look ahead for planning purposes. You can look up a future date on the human design chart makers online. Note:

Only use the **BLACK** lines/gates if you do this. Most Human Design Free Profile sites have a "Just now" type of link.

When you are using this to plan launches or programs in your business, you might look ahead to see when you have both the transit activations that will help you and correlate it to a time in your moon cycle that typically has more energy. And… if you don't have enough to track, you can add in monitoring your menstrual cycle for good measure!

REFLECTOR GOALS

A LOT GOES on tracking and observing patterns and routines that it almost seems like a big ask for Reflectors to set goals. Can I make a suggestion? Make your first goal to find some equilibrium with your energetic patterns. Make a note of the things that surprise you, learn where you have peace and ease in your business. Then, base your goals around creating more surprise, peace, and ease.

Your superpower is seeing the big picture. You can evaluate systems, communities, relationships, and even businesses. While you're getting to know your energy over the next 28-day cycle, think about what you want to create in your business. Take the next cycle to prepare and clarify what you want your community, business, and offers to look like. What would be healthy for you and your community? What do you want to change, and what is working well? Evaluate your business and life first, and then make goals to make the changes you want. The cool thing about your extended processing time is that it allows you to gather a lot of momentum in your goals.

While you're evaluating, take a look at energy leaks in your current operations. Is there something that you do that drains you? Are there opportunities for outsourcing the things that are dragging you down? One piece of your profile worth your consideration is your unconscious sun gate. In the Gene Keys system, this is called your Radiance, and it is about your health. Thinking about its shadow and gift in the light of healthy business, relationships, spirit, and body can be particularly enlightening for Reflectors.

When you do sit down to gather your thoughts about what you've made a note of, try to pick a time when you're activated favorably. Perhaps this means that the center your conscious sun gate is in is activated, or maybe you would like to plan from the perspective of a Projector. Goals can be challenging for Reflectors. Your energy is constantly changing and shifting. When you set goals, you have to commit to them. That's just how goals work. You don't have as much stability in your energy, so when you commit to something, you rely on your future energy to follow through. While this is the same as any other type, your future self has more variability than others who have definition.

The traditional goal-setting advice of setting a goal and taking massive action may not work for you. Don't feel bad. It doesn't work for most people. But, goals are an essential part of running a business. It's how we measure how well things are working and figure out the elements that need adjustment. Consider when you're creating a sales funnel. You need to put some metrics and deadlines on its performance, or you won't be able to modify or optimize it effectively. In things that have a short timeline (up to 90 days), be as specific as possible.

You also want to set a focus for each 90-day segment in your business (you might align to the quarters, but if you're going all rebel on me, set your 90 days whenever you want.) Decide what element of your business you want to grow in this time. Is it audience growth? Is it messaging alignment? Is it reach? Is it traffic to your sales page or webinar? Set a target on your 90-day goal, but realize that there will be some flexibility in that metric as you progress towards it and have more things to respond to. When you have more information, update your goals.

The problem with committing strongly to your goals in advance is that you lose your power to respond in the moment to maximize your activations. Rigid goals commit your energy in advance, leaving you tied up and unable to respond in the moment or you find that you don't actually have energy for the things you committed to. Which means set the goals. But they need to be tended to along the way. FYI, I'm speaking as a Generator that has an entirely open will center, so you may have energy elsewhere in your chart that lets you do goals a little differently. In general, when you're setting goals, keep in mind that your power is in the moment, AND you need to have some direction in your business.

I suspect that you've been burned by the typical (heavy-handed?) advice on goals in the past and are a bit hesitant even to set them. You can only have so many goals and not reach them before you start telling yourself a story about your abilities to achieve and goal setting. Be real, have you given up on goals? My advice is to shift your mindset about goals. You want to have your high-level navigational goals. The SMART goal people will probably hunt me down for this, but leave them vague. They can be dreamy and fuzzy. One of my high-level goals is to have a business that has a 2x/year launch for a signature program or mastermind and a few 1:1 clients. Traditional goal advice would want me to start filling in the details, give it a deadline and assign measurements of success. It's OK if you don't.

BUSINESS MODELS FOR REFLECTORS

BEING A NON-ENERGY TYPE, you will have to account for the inevitable highs and lows in your energy. Automation is your best friend. So is outsourcing. You want to think of ways to set your business up to make offers and accept people's money while you nap. Or, if you make your money in spurts, consider funneling some of that money into investments that make passive or semi-passive income. While you may not be on this planet to "work" like the Generators, you are here to be supported financially so you can fulfill your life's work and mission. That doesn't just happen. I mean, it kind of does once you have some momentum, but usually, you have to make some good decisions on how you set your business up and feed the money generation machine with consistent Calls to Action for your customers.

It might be the Generator in me, but I've never found there to be a truly passive source of income. Meaning you need to inject some form of energy into it to keep it going and producing. So, let's say that your offer is a course. How are you directing traffic to that course? Are there links in your automated email sequences? Do you have social media posts that

CTA to your course? Do you run ads? Do you talk about your offer often enough for your followers to know you have one?

Reflectors do best with a simple business model. Maintaining multiple offers, funnels, and accounts will be overwhelming. You are only a Manifesting Generator some of the time, OK? Remember how I talked about your environment being important? Think of your customer journey as the environment in your business. The more zen you can create here, the easier it will be to manage and maintain your business.

Your profile is like the suit you wear in your business. It is also one of the few energies that Reflectors can count on to be consistent throughout their lifetime. Lean into your profile when thinking of how to create content. For example, a 3 line will do well with sharing their experiences, while a one might do better with a teaching type post.

Setting up your business to maximize your passions is critical. You will want to find ways to do the things you love the most and outsource the things that tire or frustrate you. I want you to think for a moment about what your ideal working situation is. What type of offers appeals to you? What offers do you have now? Do they bring in a rewarding amount of money? What elements drain you? How many people do you want to work with each month? Exploring the gates of your incarnation cross (or your Gene Keys Activation Sequence) can be super powerful for a Reflector. These four gates are about the four primary gifts you have, and 2 of the 4 of them talk about purpose and life's work. Aligning your business energetically to these four keys can help create motivation and ease for you.

. . .

When you plan out how your offers fit together and into your business, you want to consider that content will fulfill different roles.

The idea of a customer journey should help your customers get to know you, trust you and be willing to pull out their wallets to purchase what you offer. You build a digital business by creating content. Of all the energy types, you may be able to batch create and pre-schedule content with the most success. But pre-scheduling content can be tricky. Live is always going to perform better than scheduled. It comes down to energy. The most exciting energy is going to be closest to your aura, so try to mix in a few lives once in a while too.

Another thing to consider: Don't re-invent the wheel with your content all the time. Observe what content gets the best engagement and re-schedule those posts. (If possible, port the comments and likes to add energetic momentum.) If you feel weird or icky about making your offer, remind yourself that you are a bad-ass mofo who all of us are waiting on to get your shit together and make an offer already. From this place of recognition of your bad-assery, create several posts that are just directing people to your offers. Get like 10 of them (the more, the better.) Put them in a scheduler on repeat, so you don't have to think about it all the time. I really like recurpost.com for this purpose because you can create decks of posts that rotate. When they get to the end, it starts at the beginning. So, make some, dump them in there. If a post flops, delete it.

There are four things that content does in your business:

1.   **Attract:** This is your freebies, social media presence, and ads. Now that you're using Human Design, you know that you are the niche that attracts your customers, so this content should represent your passions,

quirks, and values. All this content needs to do is get them interested enough to learn more.

2. **Nurture:** This content is your email sequences, social media presence, small and mid-level offers, and other valuable content. This should grow your relationship with your customer. The email sequence is where you share story, values, give away more good stuff, and prepare them to be warm when you have something to sell. This goes the same for social media. Small and mid-level offers (up to about $300) are relationship building when they buy that product and find out how amazing your stuff is, that it is perfect for them, and you are the person they want to learn from. If you do your mid-level offers well, you have customers for life.

3. **Convert:** You have to have content that asks for the sale. Which means you need to be clear about what you're selling. For me, getting clear about who I am, what I stand for, and how I want to fulfill my purpose in this world came from learning more about my energy dynamics, healing shadows, and following satisfaction. (For you, this would be surprise.) Then things clicked into place, and I didn't have to force the message out. I just had to speak words true to my energy, and people are attracted to me in weird and wonderful ways. But sales are still not something that feels natural to me. I still have to make sure that my customer journey gives people calls to action at the appropriate times to lead them towards my larger offers.

4. **Deliver:** Once you have sales, you need to deliver what you promised. Most of the time, this content feels the easiest to you. Just make sure that you use some of your energy to feed the machine and create content that does the other things too, OK?

I'd like to bust one myth that *all* you need is a high ticket offer. This seems to be the standard advice going around coaching circles. And while I agree that a high ticket offer is a good approach for most coaches and course creators, it's tough to pull off if you don't have a few other offers that build trust and feed the funnel. Sales is a numbers game. The smaller offers don't make as much money, but their purpose is to have people who will give you the time of day about your high ticket offer. The fact is that to sell a high ticket offer, you need a relationship. You build the relationship through curating a journey for your customer. Someone may skip the lower stuff and go straight to your discovery call. But, they are rarely willing to do this without the foreplay, so to speak.

ADVERTIZING FOR REFLECTORS

ADVERTIZING, like all things Reflector, is an enigma. Your aura (the energetic handshake that others perceive) is similar to a Manifestor but not as provoking. Manifestors have no trouble getting attention. Reflectors can often hide in a crowd because you are like a mirror. People notice the reflection, but not the mirror itself. Typically when you approach advertising, it is to amplify your aura so that people can get to know you exist and get a feel for what you're all about. Because your aura is more passive, this doesn't work as well as it should unless you can time the ads to your activations, which might get a little complicated. Complication is no bueno for you.

You can have ads that kill it at one time and flop another. So, it's hard to know what is actually "working" and why. The good and bad news for you is that everything goes for ads... and nothing goes for ads. In general, before you put money behind something, try testing your posts on your existing audience. Try testing it at different times in your lunar cycle. If you go to the trouble of creating something, don't assume it was bad just because it didn't work at one moment in time. Try not to take anything personally about your content, and reschedule things to try a few times before deciding their success or failure. I like **www.recurpost.com** for this reason; you can create decks that automatically repost when you get to the end. (I'm not an affiliate or anything; I just like and use their product.)

Ads are about amplifying momentum. Look at your organic posts and see what things attract the most engagement. Those are good indicators of the content that will appeal to your people. Once they are in your realm, retargeting ads are fantastic for you. Often Reflectors have the most trouble getting people into their world in the first place. I'm going to invite you to consider three things regarding ads. Play around with these types of posts and see what gives you momentum.

1.   **Boosted Post.** Yeah, yeah, yeah, I know. I've heard the naysayers that a boosted post is just helping Zuck buy his thousandth beach home. But, consider this: you need to convey your message, your truth, and attract people, and you can't if they have never seen anything you create. Consider what gets the attention of your audience in the past. That is likely the type you want to amplify with ads. If you find that some of that content is killing it in your community, that's the content that you should try to amplify with a boosted post. Find a post that had lots of engagement. I'm not talking engagement from your mom. I mean engagement from your actual target customers. When you boost it, make sure you copy the engagement (it's literally just a checkbox in ads manager.) You have your energy and the energy of people in your community that responded to the post and use that momentum to reach strangers. Make sure there is a small call to action (link to a freebie, join you on social, etc.)

2.   **Thought Reversal Ad.** This type of ad uses values to call out your ideal client. It helps them shift a belief, and because of this, it is a powerful way to attract customers. Reflectors can use value-based ads easier than other energy types. It calls out your customer without pissing them off.

. . .

How it works:

- Take an industry standard and talk about how it is the old way or the wrong way. You can pick a limiting belief, but an industry standard will help you stand out from others in your niche.
- Empathize, saying you understand why they think that way.
- Discredit the common thought or belief. Usually, this looks like pointing out the flaw in logic. Typically it goes something like this: if everyone followed that advice, we should all have full coaching schedules and full courses, and people doing other things would fail. (Be more subtle than this, please. It was for effect. Soften it with your details.)
- Illustrate the story of what happens when you stay with that type of thinking
- Call to Action to the new way

Story Ad. Think of a story that your ideal customer can empathize and relate to. (This is what they are going through right now that you can help them with.) Layer on the authority by telling them details like your experience solving this problem. Make sure you have a CTA. It isn't that different from a boosted post, in fact most of your social media posts will follow some form of storytelling, and when you add a CTA, that makes it an ad.

One place to look for inspiration (and to heal shadows) is the gate and line of your Unconscious Moon. In Gene Keys, it is the Attraction Sphere. It can give you insight into the qualities, values, and type of content that will attract your people and help build a relationship with them. It can also show you where you might need to do some healing work so that you can actually attract people from a clear frequency. Also, conscious sun gate because it's your strongest energy.

Momentum is the most important thing in attracting customers. You have your own energy and momentum, but your community and content will also create and add to it. In my opinion, this explains why the big names can do pretty much anything where advertising is concerned. They have created sufficient momentum, and their community gives them authority, adding different pieces of energy to the content, making it more appealing to a broader audience.

Building an audience becomes much easier the more people you have in your community. Once people are in your community, you can sell to them. You attract people by holding your frequency by speaking your truth loud and proud, and customers come to you. That's the secret. But, if you look for ways to amplify your momentum, that's how you get quantum results. It's about combining energy AND strategy.

MONEY IN YOUR BUSINESS

REGARDLESS OF YOUR ENERGY TYPE, you will want to have some built-in safety structures. In her book Big Magic (which should be required reading for anyone who wants to earn money off their creativity), Elizabeth Gilbert says that you need to treat your (creative project of whatever type) as a baby. You need to let it grow and learn and figure itself out before you expect it to pay the bills. Reflectors, more than any type, need stability. Stress shuts you down. So, whenever possible, it's a good idea to use your money to make more money.

I know this is counter to what you hear all over the internet: people go from nothing to 6 figures in a month. While that can happen, it's not typical, and if you're expecting your income from a new business to support you right out of the gate, it's going to put a lot of pressure on you and your creation. Do you work well under pressure? Do you love what you're doing when you're under pressure? Maybe you do, but for me, that's not the case. Diversifying your income streams is one of the best ways to create stability so that you can get your business off the ground and get through your low ebbs in energy without being stressed out or feeling like you have to do something to bring money in. Just a little disclaimer, I'm not a financial advisor and don't claim to be. Make aligned decisions about your money, and get the right professional advice. The discussion below is food for thought.

1. **Semi-passive income:** Your money is where your energy is, so "passive income" is a bit of a misnomer; you will always have to feed energy into passive income projects at times. But, it can act as a bank for Reflectors. You feed it when you have the energy, and you let it coast when you don't. Once you have a sales funnel built and a product created (for example, a course), you can turn your attention to it when it starts to underperform and feed it with your energy. You probably have many things already created that you could set up an evergreen funnel for. When you re-purpose content, make sure the product is still aligned to your message. Something else to consider is packaging some of your older stuff (or creating something especially for the purpose) into upsells, downsells, offer bumps, etc.

2. **Affiliate Marketing**: This can take a lot of work, but the way I recommend it is that you have a few products that you recommend to your audience with affiliate links. Make them part of your existing customer journey, and you can capture some profit by piggybacking on your current marketing structures. You could also consider affiliate marketing on a larger scale, for example. You sell the course or whatever it is, and someone else fulfills it. I'm sure you've seen this with the big names. If you're good at attracting people to your message but don't feel like it's the right thing to offer a signature program, this could be a good option for you. This can also be a good fit for Reflectors, who may not always have the energy to deliver certain offers, like coaching packages. Everyone is different, and it is especially true for Reflectors, so consider where your skills are and what's easy in your business. If you are great at the upfront attraction of customers but don't love delivering services, this can work

well. On the other hand, if you work better behind the scenes and attraction is a chore for you, this can be a nice addition to your own products.

3. **Investments:** Find an advisor you jive with, and let their energy manage it. One of the best financial lessons is the power of compound interest. Set a regular withdrawal, and forget about it, even if it's a small amount. Don't watch and worry about it all the time. You access it later, and it will need time to grow. Unlike property, this type of investment is usually liquid unless the fund is locked for some reason, usually tax reasons. Your advisor should help you figure out your risk tolerance and choose an investment that is right for you.

4. **Income property**: This can be a good match for Reflectors because the energy needed to maintain it is usually infrequent and sporadic, although it depends on your chosen property. Property has its own energy. So do renters. If this is an option for you, think about the logistics of the property you purchase. Are you OK with the occasional sounds, smells, and sharing of outdoor space of renting out a basement apartment? Suppose you don't live at the property. Are you willing to hire someone to manage it or be available yourself for the emergencies and maintenance that come up, usually at inconvenient times? You can rent rooms or suites via Airbnb or similar sites to earn cash and not have the long-term renter situation, but then the turnover presents another thing to manage. Another way property can make you money is by living in a place long enough to give you equity. You only access equity when you sell your home but typically re-invest it in another place to live. Equity isn't really the type of money you can rely on to provide stability unless you're willing to sell your property.

Managing your money is an important part of business. Reducing the emotional reactivity around it is typically the first and most crucial step. The majority of what I do is help people manage the emotional roller coaster of business in my small group and 1:1 containers. Find out more here: **http://carmenfarrellknapp.com/workwithme**. You want to think of ways to use your money to serve and support you rather than being at its mercy.

Signing off and a few CTA's

I have other books in this series that are the bomb once you use your strategy and authority consistently. The logical next step is the book in this series "Finding your Business Mojo with Human Design." This is where I really dive into leveraging your unique energy in your messaging and marketing. For example, where to look in your chart on who you might be best positioned to serve, how you best communicate, and how to use it to create your messaging.

Obvi, you can find me on social media. Handles change, but my name won't, so you can search me out as Carmen Farrell Knapp. I would love to hang out with you in the online world. Let me know how you're using Human Design in your business.

BOOK TWO

MANIFESTORS

NO DEFINED SACRAL CENTER, ONE OR MORE MOTOR CENTER
CONNECTED DIRECTLY OR INDIRECTLY TO THE THROAT

Manifestors

To Inform	Anger	Peace
STRATEGY	NOT SELF THEME	SELF THEME

If you are a Manifesting Generator, I'm kicking you out. Go back to the Generator section unless you're reading this because you want to better understand a Manifestor in your life. That isn't you BTW.

I know, its tough love, but I don't want you to create any bad habits right from the start. MG's are Generators, and as sexy as it is to think you're a hybrid, it will F you up, and mean massive course correction down the road. I love you, but get outta here.

Sorry, Manifestors, from here on, its all about you.

I bet if you had a penny for every time people have told you you're "too much," you'd be rich. Your aura is naturally provocative, independent, creative, and has this tendency to challenge the status quo and authority.

Your purpose in the world is to move humanity forward with your innovations. In short, you stimulate human evolution. The tribe and the collective will resist this because survival has been in the familiar ways, and there could be danger in something unknown. Usually, people don't want to change, evolve or do things in new ways unless they have to. Disrupting the status quo of the people around you can make them… edgy.

INTRODUCTION BEING A MANIFESTOR

YOU REALLY CAN BE the change you want to see in the world, and others will see you doing that and join your call to action. If you tell people what you're all about. The right people, your people, will notice what you are doing and line up to be part of your movement. You have an amazing capacity to lead, invent, innovate and get others inspired to get involved. This is necessary because you might have noticed that your follow-through game is a bit sketchy. This is OK! Generator take up where you leave off to finish what you start. You give them something to respond to so they can do the work they love doing. It also has the benefit of freeing you up to stay in the realm of ideas, potential, and creativity, which you typically like more than the monotony of actually bringing something into existence.

You are a very powerful person. So much, that it has attracted attention that has conditioned you to be something you aren't because others are uncomfortable with your shine. I know you don't need my permission, but if that's what you're waiting on, you have permission to be the bad-ass you are. Step into your shine. Stop worrying about what others will say, feel, do. That keeps you small, and you are not meant to play small. But, to play in the big leagues, you have to decide consciously and commit fiercely to you. To claim back your power, your experience, and your design. To allow yourself to align to your energy means that others will be OK with you as you actually are. Or they can peace out, and choose not to be around you. It's not easy! Your design rubs against others, so when you decide to live how you were meant to, others will be provoked.

You, my beautiful Manifestor, are a disruptor. It is a good thing! You can handle the challenges of this role, but it is not a smooth, conflict-free, people-pleasing route. The meaning you assign to conflict situations will be an important part of how you keep moving forward without getting bogged down. In business, forward momentum is critical to success. I hate to be the bearer of bad news, but you have probably noticed that often you don't even have to do or say anything for some people to take you the wrong way. Let other people be responsible for their feelings and keep your eyes on your process and contributions to the world. Own it that you are intense and not for everyone all the time.

Now that I've got that little pep talk out of the way let's talk about your childhood. I have 2 Manifestor children in my life (that I know about.) One lives part-time with his dad and part-time with his mom. His dad is very strict, controlling, and rigid. While this isn't an ideal situation for any child, for a Manifestor child, it's the worst. The weeks he is with his dad, he shuts down. He tries not to draw attention, which is hard for a Manifestor. When he inevitably does break out and do something odd, creative or quirky, he gets shot down with judgment. He has his coping mechanisms, and his mom is a block away if he just can't handle it anymore, but I can't imagine him coming out of childhood with any kind of relationship with his dad.

He blossoms into a quirky, creative, independent guy during the weeks with his mom. With increased freedom comes increased confidence. You can practically see the conditioning that makes him cautious about when he relaxes into his true self. Sometimes, I get to observe his magic when he acts impulsively without thinking about the consequences. It's like he can't help himself, and what he comes up with are the most random, beautiful things. It's also interesting to watch him with his friends. He leads with this quiet, unconscious confidence. He is going to do what he wants. If one of the guys doesn't, he has no problem going off on his own, and he can navigate this without making it a problem in his friendships. He has this confidence in what he wants that people around him find attractive.

Often with Manifestor children, they have two alternating coping mechanisms for being a square peg in a round world. Shut down, repressive, overly cautious about their ideas, often judging themselves before others can do it to them. When they are like this, they can be secretive or sneaky and not tell people what's going on with them for fear of being judged, controlled, or, worst, prevented from doing something. Then they can swing to the rebel child who cares nothing about consequences, whose feathers are ruffled, and what the outcome will be. They need to follow that inspiration no matter what. When a Manifestor child is in a bad place, you can feel their anger radiating off them.

If you are a parent to a Manifestor, it can be challenging to give them freedom to innovate, but with boundaries for safety. The strategy of informing is not about asking for permission, but in a parent-child role, the child needs to discuss first (really, ask permission,) then inform and do. I know this isn't groundbreaking parenting advice because it seems obvious that children ask permission, but for Manifestors, it is particularly important. When you establish trust with your Manifestor kid that you won't say no without reason, it helps them develop the communication skills they need to inform and be better able to operate as themselves despite the resistance of people around them. It also means that they have the opportunity to see what they are capable of. It will permit them to do weird things to explore themselves and their environment to find innovations.

The conditioning we get in childhood teaches children how to engage with our family unit and tribe. Essentially you learn how to get along and conform to the community you're born into. This socialization is essential for survival and teaching children how to be safe in the world. But, it is also something you spend adulthood healing from. Manifestors don't conform well, and they can't get through childhood without being conditioned to be a Generator: to wait, get along, and soften their energy. And it can mean they have a challenging childhood to overcome as they learn how to be a disruptor and proud of it.

I've spent so much time on your childhood because it is an important mechanic of how you show up in the world and business. You have to be in such integrity with your emotions. You already have energy that pushes against people and can trigger them, especially if you add your own wounds, stories about being repressed, controlled and scorned for doing what you're meant to do: initiate. It can be intense if you don't have good emotional boundaries. You might have a story that when you inform, it just makes people angry, so it's safer for you not to. But when you don't inform, and no one notices you trying to initiate, you get angry that no one listens. The problem is that all (bad) roads lead to anger for you. If you're not very careful with your intentions, expectations and how you assign meaning to situations that anger will come across to your potential customers and repel them. Its push energy layered on top of push energy, and no one wants to be pushed.

. . .

Taking on your shadows and wounds head-on and clearing up the disempowering stories you tell yourself is going to be the first thing you want to do before you even think about your copywriting, messaging, and marketing. You can't hide your intensity. If you're coming into your business from a wounded place of anger, desperation or have intentions other than serving your customers, it will be obvious. Other's energy isn't as direct as yours. They can hide their cracks better.

I will tell you something that I wish I knew as a child. The only person who can hurt your feelings is you. That goes both ways. You can't hurt others' feelings. Wait. What? I bet heard that you hurt others' feelings nearly every day and, it made you angry because you were just being truthful, or direct, or informing people of your intentions. How this works: there is a circumstance or stimulus in your environment. It doesn't matter what this is; the circumstance is neutral. Even if it's something "bad," it is still only negative when your thoughts get involved in assigning meaning. Whatever your thoughts are about the circumstance will trigger emotions. Negative meaning = negative emotion. Emotions are what will drive speaking and acting. If you have negative emotions driving your actions, your results are likely not what you want.

You are 100% responsible for your thoughts, meanings, feelings, actions, and results. You are 0% responsible for someone else's feelings. That's on them. Now, this doesn't give you license to be a dick, but when you are doing your thing, informing and initiating, and it triggers people, it's not yours to take on. You do not need to assign the meaning that your actions were bad because someone had a feeling. The more you can let go of the people who aren't ready for your message will open you up to those who are. Who can maybe only respond to you (Generators and Reflectors,) or are waiting for an invitation to your world (Projectors,) or are initiated themselves by your ideas (Manifestors.) I mean, you come up with some pretty crazy and amazing shit! Don't hide that away just because you're scared of hurting feelings. It doesn't make you callous or selfish. It makes you a responsible adult with good emotional boundaries who can handle themselves no matter what the circumstance.

As you start to put down all of the things you think you should be, all of other people's opinions of what you should do, how you should act, speak, be, all of a sudden, the anger lifts. Your aura lightens and brightens, and the customers who are meant for your magic come out of the woodwork. Your natural process of initiating and informing becomes irresistible. People notice for all the right reasons. When you reach out to someone from a place of service and offer what you can do for them, that natural pushing energy from your aura inspires them to action. Not inspires them to ghost you.

Your process starts with inspiration. You are the only energy type that can initiate their own process by going out and looking for inspiration. It's still not truly internal, though. You still need that spark from spirit, source, or the universe, but it happens quickly. Everyone else has to wait for a sign to initiate them. Your environment inspires you, and immediately you go to work (provided you use your authority to know that it is the right thing for you), gather resources, get your brain churning, and feed your own process.

This is going to jump-start your creative flow, which is usually a pretty focused and intense time of working out the details of a situation and weaving in your unique perspective. If someone interrupts you in your flow, you can find it very irritating. This is why informing people is so important for you. Your magic is putting your spin on something to develop something new and innovative.

. . .

If you take an online course, you probably aren't the type to go through it methodically. You will take the ideas in a course and create a whole new system that works for you. Often with Manifestors, you will see them take a concept, then go into their cave for a while and emerge with a brilliant spin or something completely new. Then they come back for more inspiration, then go and create, and the cycle continues. When you go into a learning process, trust that your ideas will be the value you get out of it, not the process or system. You're looking to be inspired and do your own thing. That includes this book! Be inspired, but make it your own.

Even Manifestors respond to their environment; they just engage with the stimulus differently than Generators. Your inspiration will be more immediate, giving you the capacity to act directly on the things your authority tells you are right for you. Essentially you go out and make it happen. You don't have to wait like a Generator does for the resources to come to them; you go out into the world and source them.

Strategy: To Initiate and Inform

Initiating is pretty straightforward. Something in your environment sparks interest for you, that inspires your creative flow. Once you are initiated, you use your authority to decide whether to spend your energy on that thing, or pass. You also initiate others process by using the other part of your strategy: informing. A bigger part of operating in alignment with your strategy is informing. Initiating happens fairly naturally, you decide whether it is right for you, then you have to tell people, which is not always easy for you.

Your strategy does not come naturally to you. Telling people what you're working on? Please. Who has time for that when you're in your groove?

Informing will rally the troops and give them time to respond to your ideas. Your energy is best used for that initial push to get something started and off the ground. It needs the energy of others to grow and thrive. If you skip informing people, you will put all your efforts into launching something, with no one there to notice it. How infuriating.

Your purpose on earth is to understand your impact on the other. This is different from Generators or Reflectors, who understand themselves and act as a beacon. You and Projectors are here to understand yourself through the other. You are going to have an impact on everyone around you. It's just who you are. Even if you wanted to be a wallflower, you can't. Your energy speaks louder than you.

Your question before doing things is, "Who and how do my actions impact?" Those are the ones you need to inform. You can come off as super impulsive and piss people off if you don't let people know ahead of time. This can be OK, their emotions are on them, but if you want to have customers in your business, you need to keep this top of mind that they need to be in on the lead-up, the process, and not just the final product.

Impact without informing will cause chaos wherever you go, so keep talking about what you are doing. It primes the pump so that when you are ready to release your new program, launch your product or take on clients, they are there waiting and already know what you're about. It also keeps the people in your circle (family, friends, and customers) in the loop so that when you pivot or change course (even in a minor way), they don't think it's coming out of left field.

Even if you have been planning and working on something for a while, people around you will probably be surprised and irritated by sudden shifts unless you tell them about it along the way. I don't mean that you mention it once in an email. I mean, talk about it frequently—conversations with eye contact.

The reason informing is so essential is to prevent anger on both sides of a relationship. Other people (even other Manifestors) can't read your energy. It is obscure, dense, and intense. People notice when you enter a room, but they may not get a good read off of you, your intentions, and how you might react. It is a provoking type of energy. If you are experiencing anger, you're not hiding it well. Especially to people with undefined solar plexus (emotional) centers who pick up on that and amplify it at 200%. That's uncomfortable for anyone, especially considering the conditioning and socialization we have about anger, particularily in women.

Of all the types, you will need to get good at managing, regulating, and feeling your emotions. This doesn't mean going on a rant to your community. It is a private practice of emotional management. You identify what you're feeling, observe what you are making it mean, and feel it as a vibration in the body.

By informing, you give people a chance to get out of your way or get on board with what you will do.

So, this looks like open lines of communication to make sure you are informing and informed of your day-to-day life and relationship. The people outside of your close bubble, you inform of the medium to big things. Informing in your business is much different in your intimate relationships. Your customers don't need a running commentary on the minor working of your business, but they will need to know what the keynotes are and what direction you are heading in.

. . .

Informing is not asking for permission. Informing comes after the decision is made. Depending on what that action looks like, your informing is of what your intentions are in using the energy of inspiration. People may not recognize it as informing, and assume you want their input, opinion, or ideas. Don't get mad at them. But, if they bring up something worth considering, check it against your authority. If it is still a correct decision for you (which is probably is if you're following strategy and authority), carry on.

Informing goes both ways. You want to know what's going on and why. You want to be informed of the plan in your household and don't like being surprised by a commitment or someone expecting you to do something without knowing why, when, and being part of the decision-making process. In relationships, you will need to keep your people in the know about your process, what you're working on, what you need from them, how things are progressing, etc. Letting your people know that you're working on something and that you need some space to do so will be much easier than snapping at them when they interrupt you at a crucial moment.

What this might look like in your business is setting guidelines and boundaries around your clients and staff, informing you of their progress, if they hit a snag, and if they will miss a deadline or expectation. It will help to be clear about your expectations in your business relationships, but be aware that not every energy type will read all the fine print (Manifesting Generators in particular.)

You're going to be sensitive to being controlled, manipulated, or not told the whole story.

.   .   .

Good lines of communication will go a long way to helping you and those around you live in harmony. When things go a little sideways, as they always do with human interaction, try to assume the best of people. Most of the time, people are just off in their own world, dealing with their stuff, and taking everything personally will be a rabbit hole of anger for you. You can't control the people around you, and it is fruitless to try. Shadow work about wanting to control everything comes up for a lot of Manifestors.

One practice that can be good for your morning routine is to take the things that are irritating you and make their meaning neutral. For example, a customer is asking for a refund on a product. They signed the refund policy, used the product, got value out of it, and now are saying they will cancel the charge on the credit card (and slander you with bad reviews) if you don't refund them. Instead of assigning the meaning that they are just out to take advantage, you can enter into a dialogue with them from a better place if you assume that the request is from a place that you don't understand and they are not a bad person. Plus, you are making sales if you're getting a refund request, so yay. While the outcome may not change, neutralizing the meaning you assign will stop you from going down the spiral of anger. It allows you to put the results into perspective and move on rather than getting caught in un-resourceful thinking.

AUTHORITY FOR MANIFESTORS

AUTHORITY IS DETERMINED BY THE CENTER(S) YOU HAVE DEFINED

AUTHORITY FOR MANIFESTORS

EMOTIONAL AUTHORITY (51% of the population)

This is the most common authority. About 50% of the population has an emotional authority. While common, most people are unaware of how to use the information and fuel that a defined solar plexus can give you. It is an awareness center for emotional processing and one of the 4 "motors" in the body graph. Using this authority takes time to process emotions, and you guessed it, awareness of the highs and lows of the wave.

Emotional authority is NOT figuring out how you feel about a decision and making decisions based on emotion.

It is about using the different emotions of your emotional wave as information to come to clarity. You feel your way through the highs and lows of emotions about that decision until you just know what the right path is. You are trying to answer the question "Is my energy available for this?"

The emotional wave is a mechanical process. You will have a stimulus that you respond to that triggers an emotion that you follow through the high, low, and between. This isn't avoidable. You will have an emotional wave regardless. You can suppress or enhance emotion, but it happens whether you want to experience it or not.

The best-case scenario is that you learn to use emotion as the experience and tool it is for you and then allow it to flow through you. Emotions can get stuck when you try to repress them, creating an elongated wave. Part of your routine should be to feel the emotions of that moment and see if you can discern where you are resisting emotion. Allow yourself to feel in a safe space if there are emotionally unresolved feelings.

The thing with emotion is that your mind and ego will want to get involved and label it as good or bad, this or that, and you will start to create stories around the emotional experience. Ego wants to move you out of discomfort as quickly as possible, but much of your growth as an entrepreneur will come from your superpower of being able to ride out the wave of discomfort. If you can learn not to identify with your emotions and mine the truth they have to tell you, then you will be unstoppable! Much of this work is awareness about what you make your emotions mean and allowing them to flow without creating resistance.

The key with the emotional wave is to make sure you have come to neutral before deciding. Does this mean you need to ride out the emotional wave on every decision? NO! But be aware of when you feel triggered (high or low) and wait until you have more emotional clarity. Most people can understand not deciding from a low part of the wave, but it's equally important to avoid the high state. Think of a time when you've been super excited about something. You commit on the spot and find that after, when you aren't on the top of the wave, you don't actually have the energy, or it is something that you aren't that passionate about, but... you said yes and are stuck seeing it through.

Depending on which channel(s) are defined for you will give your wave a different flavor. You can experience the wave through different channels in their own way. The type of wave will also determine what you are available to direct your energy towards. Decisions of this nature will need time to process and ride out the wave, as these are the types of decisions that will have the most power for you. Not everything that inspires you is super important, but the things that are hardwired to initiate your creative process are determined by the active channels in your authority.

While your strategy is to initiate, your authority will tell you if you have the energy available for it. Unlike a splenic authority which is a clear yes or no, you will rarely be 100% sure because you have to feel out the decision through the high and low and everything in between your emotional wave. So for you, pretty sure is good enough. Be aware of when your mind starts to try to sway you one way or another. Stick with the feeling you get from a decision, not the thoughts, stories, and drama.

The solar plexus is an awareness center for emotional energy. You will experience emotional energy in a specific, defined way. It will be unique to you but reliable, consistent, and predictable. You will seek things out that give you an emotional experience because this is part of how you experience the world, learn, and grow. If you have this center defined, you are here to live a robust, vibrant, and varied emotional life. Your inner authority will respond to the experiences, relationships, and things that let you play out the emotional experience. But, your emotional wave won't respond to *every* stimulus. The type of circuitry will give you a clue as to what you are hardwired to respond to in life (see the types of waves for more on that specifically.) But, your authority will give you a yes or a no, not a why. Your mind and ego will not be satisfied. So, there is a practice of quieting the mind in following your authority.

Your emotions enhance your life, and you can utilize the energy of emotion to create. Social pressure means most of us view emotion as something to be restrained, resisted, or, worst case, be ashamed of. It can be a completely new concept to allow emotion to have the deciding vote in how you do life.

The first step is to start to become aware of your emotions because you probably feel more than you're consciously aware of. Notice if a specific emotion signals the start of your wave. Observe how you move through your wave with different triggers. Start to develop your vocabulary on your emotions, and notice the nuances between similar emotions. Journaling can help with this. Another technique is to check in with yourself at each meal, morning and night, and notice what you feel. The more awareness you bring to your emotions, the better you will understand how to work with this powerful, amazing energy.

Here are a few things to keep in mind when working with emotional energy:

- An emotion is just a vibration in the body. Some of the more intense emotional energy like anxiety, or even excitement, will pass through you. The chemical spike an emotion creates in your blood lasts approximately 90 seconds. So, if you can stay with the feeling, observing yourself and breathing through it, it will flow through you. If you resist or fight emotion, that spike can extend, or worse, rebound with more intensity.

- Most of working with emotional energy is learning not to resist. Allow it to flow, observe how you feel through the whole experience, come to neutral, then act. Resistance can cause your emotional energy to get stuck, and this is how you can potentially experience extended times in lower vibration emotions like depression.
- Avoid labelling emotions as positive or negative. The energy of emotion is neutral until you assign meaning to it with thoughts. You are designed to experience the whole range of emotions, not just the "positive" ones. Taking the mindset of observing the sensation of emotions in your body will help.

When you are around people without definition in the solar plexus, they will pick up on your emotional wave (whether they know it or not!) and amplify it back to you. While you can share your emotions with others, your emotional wave is yours, and if you are trying to work through something, it is best to do it out of the energy of others.

Types of Emotional Wave

The Source of all Waves: Solar Plexus to Sacral: 6-59: Channel of Intimacy

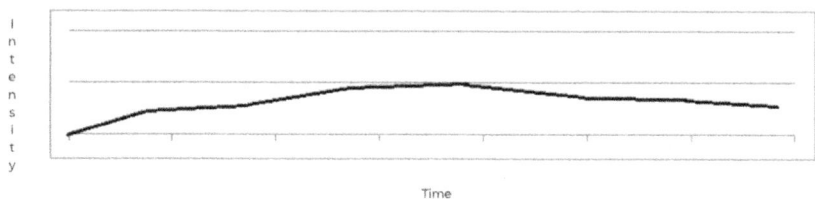

Source of all Waves

Solar Plexus to Sacral Center. 6-59 Channel of Intimacy

The source of all waves is about the intimacy in relationships that allows people to create something new. It will respond to relationships that can lead to the creativity to build or create. The channel is called the channel of mating, or intimacy, and can refer to creating new life or any other creative process between 2 people.

This wave responds to the things that create a connection between people. It will flow up then plateau with each connection. It is a gentle rise, plateau, then drift back down. The theme is about human connection, responding to relationships, and seeking out the connections that will lead to something new. It is a reasonably gentle wave and very good at relating to others. Anyone with this channel will be a Generator and will want to follow the relationships that lead them to create things they are passionate about.

. . .

Tribal Wave: Solar Plexus to Root: 49-19: Channel of Synthesis and Solar Plexus to Heart: 37-40: Channel of Community

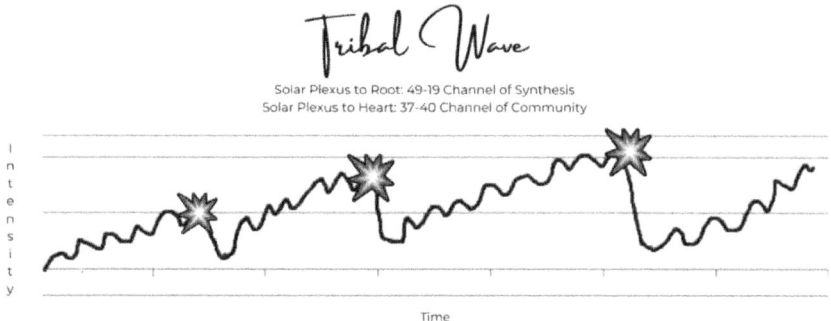

The tribal wave will respond to survival or need in the intimate community. It is part of the tribal circuitry. It responds to the needs of the tribe or family (tribal is different from collective, which is concerned with the greater good, tribal is concerned with the survival and thriving of people in the close circle.) It is concerned with resources and providing the tools you and your tribe need to survive.

Physical connection is a key component to this wave, and when you are triggered, it will help you ground yourself to connect physically. It operates like a ratchet. You are triggered, then relax back, kind of like you shake it off. It may take a few times before you reach the explosion point, but you will eventually get agitated enough by the trigger to have a release of emotion. Then there will be a reset. This wave is not subtle and can feel a bit out of control at times. Being aware of how this wave operates and your typical responses will help you find positive ways to release the emotional energy. Do you pick a fight so that you can hug it out? Perhaps it would be easier to ask for a hug. Just sayin'

. . .

The Individual Wave: Solar Plexus to Root: 55-39:Channel of Emoting, Solar Plexus to Throat 22-12: Channel of Openness

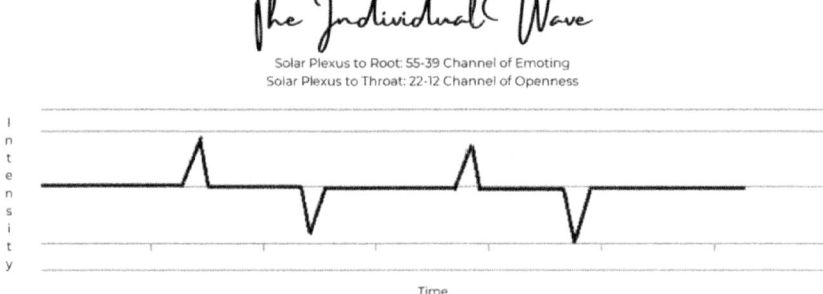

Solar Plexus to Root: 55-39 Channel of Emoting
Solar Plexus to Throat: 22-12 Channel of Openness

The individual wave is characterized by passion. Your mood is how you express this wave. It can be a moody wave, and at times you will want to share this emotion with others, and at times it is best kept just for your experience alone. It has peaks then comes back to steadiness, then it drops, then comes back to steady. You want to be conscious of when you need time alone to feel your emotions without the influence of others. This will help you avoid getting trapped in the lows and keep moving with the mood. It is important to allow yourself space, connect to your needs and desires, and learn how to ground yourself when it gets a little too wavy. The channels of this wave are part of the individual circuitry and will respond to the things that help you grow and advance as an individual.

The Abstract Wave: Solar Plexus to Root: 30-41: Channel of Recognition, Solar Plexus to Throat: 36-35: Chanel of Transitoriness

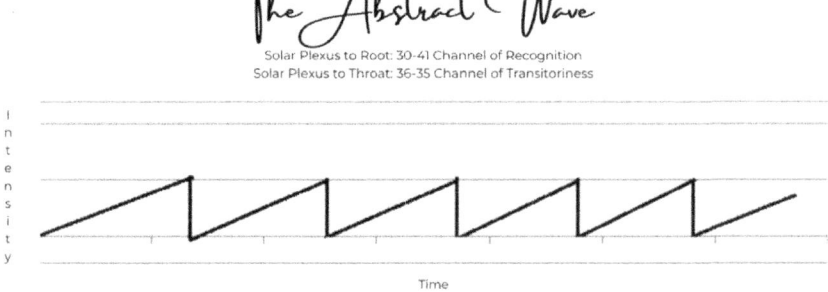

Solar Plexus to Root: 30-41 Channel of Recognition
Solar Plexus to Throat: 36-35 Channel of Transitoriness

There will be a gentler rhythm to this wave than the individual wave. It will ebb and flow by responding to experience. The two channels associated with this wave carry a great deal of friction. The 35-36 seeks new beginnings and wants to respond to the things worth pursuing, and the 30-41 communicates the lessons learned through overcoming friction through emotion. Remember that this is your natural energetic state, so following strategy and authority and allowing this wave to operate as it is meant to will help you determine the conflict that is worthwhile for you and holds the vision and optimism that each experience brings. This wave can present challenges when you enter into an experience with an expectation that is not met, causing an emotional crash. It is important not to attach yourself to an outcome Rather, you are going into an experience for the sake of the emotion it will create and the things you can learn from it.

Splenic Authority (9 % of the population)

The spleen is all about intuition, survival, and the physical body. Intuition can have many voices, and getting to know the communication from your authority is key. You might even have conditioning around "intuition" and what it means to be intuitive. As the Spleen is responsible for survival (both as an individual and of the tribe), you will be sensitive to situations that trigger your spidy sense about how viable, healthy or beneficial something is for you or the community.

A Manifestor with Splenic Authority has the quickest moving energy of any type/authority combination. You can bring your ideas and creations to life very quickly. You are inspired, the spleen gives you an immediate yes/no and you go do. Everyone else has to wait in some form, whether that is for something for their strategy to respond to, or wait out their authority to give them the go ahead.

The typical description of splenic authority is that you have an inner knowing of what is right or wrong for you. Oh yeah, that makes it totally clear (that was sarcasm in case the written word failed to communicate the nuance.) Welcome to life with a splenic authority. There is a physical sensation to this "knowing." But, it can be subtle, and the splenic authority will only answer once, so if you're not paying attention at that moment, you can miss the cue.

For you, more than any other authority type, you will need to find ways to stay present in the moment and grounded in your body.

. . .

Your mind will try to override the splenic decisions by using logic. Remember the role of the mind as an external authority. Getting out of your head and into your body is the only way to hear the intuitive hit of the spleen. Many splenic authorities will find meditation or another form of grounding and centering practice helpful to tune into the physical sensations. It also gives you space to observe thoughts and all the tricky ways they try to manipulate your decisions. You want to feel the difference between mind/thought/ego energy and your splenic intuition. Eckhart Tolle's "The Power of Now" is a compelling book for you, and I strongly recommend reading it. Several times.

Each of the gates of the spleen has its own flavor or sensation. Some of the gates will have a physical sensation, and all of them have a fundamental fear associated with it. I like to flip the narrative about the fear gates of the spleen and choose to think of them as indicators of the things your energy is available for. They create a theme in your life that gives you purpose and can reveal some of your core values. For example, gate 18's association is a fear of authority. This might indicate that you value freedom or have a purpose of questioning or challenging authority. It also might be a theme in your life to overcome your fear of power and something you can help others do.

I want to let you decide what they mean to you, but I hope you lean into creating meaning that supports you. I'm going to run through the gates of the spleen and what some of the connections are. Look at where you have definition in the spleen, and which one(s) create channels. I've included the shadow and gifts of these gates, taken from Richard Rudd's Gene Keys, so you can use it as a litmus test of how you are expressing the energy. Ideally, you want to express the high-frequency energy of the gate rather than indulging fear. If the gate is linked to one of the senses, I have also included it. This may help you zero in on how your spleen communicates.

. . .

Gate 18: Fear of Authority.

Shadow: Victim mindset- All judgment is self-judgment, and the level you identify with your judgments is the degree of resistance you will create.

Gift: Integrity: You have a knack for testing the integrity of people and your environment to determine what needs to evolve.

Physical sensation: Touch. You can determine the physical strength of structures at a vibrational level. There may be a tactile element to your splenic communication.

Gate 28: Fear of Death

Shadow: Purposelessness (fear that you will die without finding your purpose)

Gift: Totality (Trust in the process of life, *despite* fear)

Physical sensation: Sound vibration. Your inner knowing may have an auditory quality to it eg, ringing in the ears or hearing your guidance as voices or conversations. You may hear phrases or conversations, or other noises as your spleen tries to communicate. Watch for patterns in your inner dialogue.

Gate 32: Fear of Failure

Shadow: Failure (Seeing learning as failure) This also has roots in the collective fear for survival as a species. The fear of being ostracized from the group literally meant death. There is an element of social fear expressed in this gate. Translated into modern times, survival = money for many people

Gift: Preservation (knowing what is worth preserving and what can be let go to evolve) Also, very good at sensing which relationships will lead to growth.

Sensation: Breath/breathing. This gate is about support and survival, and breath is the most fundamental resource for survival. Observe your breath when you are listening to your splenic authority. If you hold your breath or speed up, it may give you clues.

Gate 44: Fear of the Past

Shadow: Interference (this is an abstract one, but I like to think of it as clearing out the karma, patterns, and programming interfering with expressing ourselves at a high frequency.)

Gift: Teamwork

Sensation: Sense of smell. You can smell the people, situations, and destiny right for you. You are a genius at reading people. You will probably instinctually know who feels right for you.

Gate 48: Fear of inadequacy

Shadow: Inadequacy (this is the root of all fears, and shadow that we are inherently inadequate)

Gift: Resourcefulness

Sensation: You can "see" the answer through the darkness. Your spleen may communicate with flashes or insights in a visual way. Notice what you are drawn to and what aesthetically appeals to you.

Gate 50: Fear of responsibility

Shadow: Corruption (This can refer to political and social corruption, but it also refers to how energetic expression can be corrupted by fear, ego, and the mind that restricts evolution and growth.)

Gift: Equilibrium (Sense of balance and cosmic order to the world)

Sensation: While not a physical sensation per sea, those with this gate have a sense of equilibrium or balance. It may be that you have a feel for when something is "off."

Gate 57 Fear of the Future

Shadow: Unease (pervasive sense that something terrible is coming, pessimism)

Gift: Intuition

Sensation: Hearing. You have a sense of interpreting what people are really saying. You can hear the nuances in sound that others may not be as sensitive to.

Ego Manifested Authority

If this is your authority, there are only a few ways it can play out. Your heart center is either directly connected to the throat through the 21-45 channel, or it goes indirectly to the throat through the g-center then up to the throat. You won't have definition in the emotional, sacral, root or splenic centers, the centers responsible for much of the physical and grounding energy in the body graph. Sometimes, it may be hard to remember that you are a *physical being* having a spiritual experience because most of your energy is a bit… abstract.

. . .

The heart center has to do with will and self-worth. The throat is about self-expression and communication. The other centers that you may or may not have defined are the identity center, having to do with love and direction, and the mental centers (Head and Anja), which deal with thought and conceptualization. It's different than the earthy, rooting, physical energy of the sacral, spleen, and root. Just like many Projectors and Reflectors, you may find physical or mindfulness practices helpful to anchor you into your physical body. That is what listening to your authority is all about. Your spiritual self communicates through your physical body, not the mind.

It will be imperative to know how your inner authority speaks to you and learn how to sort out when you are being pulled towards making not-self decisions. Part of your process is to talk it out with people to figure out what is right for you. What you are trying to determine with these conversations is what do you *want?* You may experience a sensation around your heart when you come to clarity on your desires. Your heart's desires are what lead you in life.

Your desires are the guideposts for you. I can already hear the conditioning coming up around "selfishness." Notice that as the BS it is. You process through your own experiences, not through the experiences of others. Your desires are what will lead you in the right direction. The conversations you have are a sounding board to help you understand your desires.

Like all authorities that need to speak it out, it's essential to have people in your life who are good at listening, holding up the mirror for you, and not giving advice unless asked. If you don't have anyone else around, you can talk to yourself, the dog, plants, whatever. You want to actually express it as sound so you can listen to your own voice. Journaling is another way to get your thoughts out of your head so you can see what you are really trying to say. Read out your words so you can hear your thoughts. Get a voice memo app for using on the go.

Your voice is so powerful. The Will center's motor fuels it. Your voice is the tool you use to make things happen in your life. Once you know your direction, the voice sets your vibrational tone that the universe matches. This is why you need to inform people of your plans and inspirations. It's your song with the universe that helps you co-create everything you want in life.

Signature: Peace Not-Self Theme: Anger

Your signature is how you know you are on the right path. When you feel peaceful, it means you are following your strategy and making decisions from your authority. This is a good health check for your energy. If you are experiencing more Anger than Peace, you want to look at how you are making decisions and where you might be operating from conditioning and/or not-self.

Peace is also where your money is. It means you are operating in alignment with your purpose, prosperity, and energy. Peace is the vibration you emit to the universe to draw in all the delicious things in the world. This is how you know you have your vibration set to the right frequency, so follow the peace in your life and business, and money will be there.

Peace is the sensation of having used your energy successfully. For Manifestors, this means you impacted the people in your world today. The word peace probably has associations for you that aren't quite what Ra was talking about when he identified this as your signature. Try borrowing the Generator signature of satisfaction and mix it in with your concept of peace. Does that help you feel the vibration of peace? You're looking for a physical sensation in the body.

In my experience, your purpose and how you fulfill it is pretty damn peaceful. If you're curious about your purpose, check out the gates of your Incarnation Cross found in your conscious and unconscious sun and earth.

MANIFESTOR GOALS

MANIFESTORS HAVE two things guiding their goals: peace and impact. Peace is not about achieving an arbitrary number. However, Manifestors of all the energy types can benefit from identifying the details that help you measure what is working and what isn't. It is more about a feeling. How can you use your energy to feel peaceful?

What types of people do you want to work with that will enhance your sense of peace? What things lead to anger or irritation? Do you feel like your business model leads to peace? Do you know what type of financial situation will allow you to feel peaceful? Do you like what you're doing? What parts of your work do you not like doing? Do you pull yourself back from having the impact you know you can have? When was the last time you felt you made an impact with your marketing? Messaging? Offers? Community?

How did that feel? Where do you feel the sensation of impact in your body? If the anger and judgment of others wasn't an issue, what would you want to do? These are essential questions for a Manifestor to reflect on. They will give you some direction when you set goals.

You have a motor connected to the throat. This means consistent energy is supplied to the center that manifests your reality and communicates with the world. When you put your energy into it, you will manifest your goals naturally, without effort, and most of the time, much quicker than other energy types. Your energy is literally meant to take form. Your goals are like a funnel directing that energy (think impact) towards the neck. Gravity naturally takes over and makes it happen. You will want to use your detail-oriented mind to try to push or force it. Use that brilliant brain of yours to find evidence that it is on its way, and track the wins, no matter how small.

The rest of the world is a little jealous of you. The traditional goal-setting (and business) advice typically works well for Manifestors because they usually go along with your strategy of initiating. Google SMART goals if you want structure to set up your goals. Keep in mind you're going to get the most out of goals that aim for impact and peace.

BUSINESS MODELS FOR MANIFESTORS

MANIFESTORS ARE fantastic at getting things going. You initiate businesses, processes, people's transformation and more. You will need to have a lead generation machine to support your business so that you can stay in your creative flow. There is some up-front work to set up the back end of your business that collects leads and takes them through a customer journey. Part of the journey is to invite them to follow you on social, where you share the details about your creative innovations in real-time. That's what will build the trust, so they buy from you. As a coach or course creator, there is a dance between automation and exposure to your exciting energy.

As a Manifestor, there are a few ways to create the support of a good back end. Hehehe. If it is possible to hire a VA, even part-time, who likes to take care of all the follow-through and support your customers that's ideal. If it isn't the right time to hire, consider seeing if there is someone in your circle (groups you belong to, for example) who could do a service exchange for setting up some web pages, funnels, and email sequences.

You can also do it yourself, but be aware of when it is irritating you to do that work and find the right time and flow. When you're working in your strategy and authority, there is serendipity to the people who find you. Still, you will also want to make sure you create the types of funnels and sequences to support your lead generation and follow-up processes so they can even out and maximize your income.

Many Manifestors do well with creating businesses, getting them off the ground and then selling them to someone who will do the follow-up and day-to-day. This means you continuously operate in your creative flow and initiate without following it up with the grunt work. I think there is a lot of conditioning around the value of "hard work" and "seeing things through" that may give you pause. That's Generator speak, and you don't have to subscribe to it. It might be the Generator in me, but I've never found there to be a truly passive source of income.

Meaning you need to inject some form of energy into it to keep it going and producing. So, let's say that your offer is a course. How are you directing traffic to that course? Are you informing people of it? Often? Have you been telling people about it for a while?

Because while you are amazing at initiating if it comes as a surprise to people, it may put them off. Are there links in your automated email sequences? Do you have social media posts that CTA to your course? Do you run ads? Do you talk about your offer often enough for your followers to know you have one?

Pre-scheduling content can be tricky. Live is always going to perform better than scheduled. It comes down to energy. The most stimulating energy is going to be closest to your aura. Your most exciting energy will be in initiating, innovating, and informing. It is probably not in spending all your time marketing yourself unless that's part of your niche. You are going to do best following your excitement and creative flow. But, how do you get clients? You focus on being the badass you are and attracting clients, which is in your wheelhouse, and create an automated back end that does the follow-up for you.

Don't re-invent the wheel with your content all the time. Observe what content gets the best engagement and re-schedule those posts. (If possible, port the comments and likes to add energetic momentum.) If you feel weird or icky making your offer, remind yourself that you are a bad-ass mofo who all of us are waiting on to get your shit together and make an offer already. From this place of recognition of your own bad-assery, create several posts that are just directing people to your offers. Get like 10 of them (the more, the better.) Put them in a scheduler on repeat, so you don't have to think about it all the time. I like **www.recurpost.com** for this purpose because you can create decks of posts that rotate. When they get to the end, it starts at the beginning. So, make some, dump them in there. If a post flops, delete it. Then all you have to deal with is your live content each week, which will be sharing your creative process and the things you're excited about.

Setting up your business to maximize your passions is critical. I want you to think for a moment about what your ideal working situation is. You will feel peaceful when you impact the right people in the right way. Peace is where it's at for you. Your ideal customers, offers, and financial success will come from the things that give you peace. Following your energy of strategy and authority will get you in the vicinity of peace, and your micro-adjustments will find the bull's eye.

· · ·

What type of offers do you feel peaceful about? What offers do you have now? Is your business financially successful, and in what ways? What elements are not so successful? How many people do you want to work with each month? Are there patterns to when you have a surge of energy?

When you plan out how your offers fit together and into your business, you want to consider that content will fulfill different roles.

The idea of a customer journey should help your customers get to know you, trust you and be willing to pull out their wallets to purchase what you offer.

There are four things that content does in your business:

1. **Attract:** This is your freebies, social media presence, and ads. Now that you're using Human Design, you know that you are the niche that attracts your customers, so this content should represent your passions, quirks, and values. All this content needs to do is get them interested enough to learn more.
2. **Nurture:** This content is your email sequences, social media presence, small and mid-level offers, and other valuable content. This should grow your relationship with your customer. The email sequence is where you share story, values, give away more good stuff, and prepare them to be warm to when you have something to sell. This goes the same for social media. Small and mid-level offers (up to about $300) are relationship building when they buy that product and find out how amazing your stuff is, that it is perfect for them, and you are the person they want to learn from. If you do your mid-level offers well, you have customers for life. When creating this content, consider how you can share your

creative process and inform your customers of what you're doing and what you have to offer. Can you use this content to initiate your customers towards small transformations to get them interested in more?

3. **Convert:** You have to have content that asks for the sale. Which means you need to be clear about what you're selling. For me, getting clear about who I am, what I stand for, and how I want to fulfill my purpose in this world came from learning more about my energy dynamics, healing shadows, and following satisfaction (I'm a Generator, and this is my version of peace.) Then things clicked into place. I didn't have to force the message out. I just had to speak words true to my energy, and people are attracted to me in weird and wonderful ways. But sales are still not something that feels natural to me. I still have to make sure that my customer journey gives people calls to action at the appropriate times to lead them towards my larger offers. This content is necessary, and you have to be deliberate about it. People don't buy if you don't tell them you have stuff for sale. So, create content that directs people to your sales page, ok?

4. **Deliver:** Once you have sales, you need to deliver what you promised. Most of the time, this content feels the easiest to you. It's probably why you became a coach or course creator in the first place. Just make sure that you use some of your energy to feed the machine and create content that does the other things too, OK?

I'd like to bust one myth that *all* you need is a high ticket offer. This seems to be the standard advice going around coaching circles. And while I agree that a high ticket offer is a good approach for most coaches and course creators, it's tough to pull off if you don't have a few other offers that build trust and feed the funnel. Sales is a numbers game. The smaller offers don't make as much money, but their purpose is to have people who will give you the time of day about your high ticket offer. The fact is that to sell a high ticket offer, you need a relationship. You build the relationship through building the journey with a customer. Someone may skip the lower stuff and go straight to your discovery call. But, they are rarely willing to do this without the foreplay, so to speak.

ADVERTIZING FOR MANIFESTORS

YOU DON'T HAVE any trouble getting attention. You have a motor to the throat, and can communicate easily with your audience. You will probably have the most success with ads to a cold audience of all the energy types. Where you are going to struggle more is the follow-up—nurturing your customers towards a higher ticket item with your customer journey. Your advertising dollars will go towards emphasizing the momentum you already have, so if you know there is ease in getting attention, get as many people into the top of your sales funnel as you can. They will sort themselves out who's for you and not, but you want the numbers on the front end. Your follow-up will be to invite them to your other content that keeps them on the cutting edge of what you're doing. Don't worry about the ones who self-select out of your group. Repelling customers is just as important as attracting them.

You can engage with your potential customers more directly and in a straightforward way than other energy types. The different types will need more relationship building before their CTA's will work. Ads to a cold audience that are direct to a sale may take a bit of finesse but can work for you. Other energy types don't have a chance with this type of ad. For perspective, the other energy types would use advertising to build relationship, and once someone is a warm audience member, they can ask for the sale, which works for you as well, but not *always* necessary. Retargeting ads are good but will be a secondary part of your advertising strategy.

The higher the ticket items will always need some form of relationship building. Still, your sales funnel can be more direct like a self-liquidating funnel for example. You would have a series of 3 products that increase in value as they progress through your funnel. The first product in a SLO funnel is a small price point like $17-$47. You will have better luck with this type of funnel on a cold audience than any other type. But, before you go saying that you can throw that whole Know-Like-Trust thing out the window, all sales will take some form of relationship, especially the high ticket ones, so don't rely too heavily on ads. You have to work harder to gain the trust factor than most because you're intense. So, using some small ticket items and over-delivering can be a way to build that trust towards higher sales.

Details are your best friend. It is (usually) aligned in your messaging to share the details with your community. If the other types had a detailed syllabus on their sales page, it would be a total mismatch. You can (usually) do that, and your community wants all the details from you. You can also share these details in your email sequences and social media content and have it feel more aligned to your energy.

The good news for you is basically anything goes with ads. You can create stories, amplify authority, boost posts that do well, make slight of mouth videos. The advertising world is your oyster. If there is a template out there, chances are you will be able to modify it for your needs, as the typical advertising and business strategies will align with your natural strategy of initiating. Any of the typical advice on ads will apply to you, so… Google.

I want to talk about a strategy that you hear a lot in the interwebs for coaches where you directly message your potential customers. Or reach out to people who are not known to you to be part of their world, for example, being a guest for their community. If this feels aligned, it can be an incredible way to spread your message and make contacts. When you consider cold contacting, you want to make sure your intention is about creating a relationship, not sales. When you reach out, you offer them something you can help them with. On the other end, it will feel pretty skeevy if it is a thinly veiled sales pitch.

A variation on this theme is to join a bunch of groups on Facebook in your niche and comment on people's messages until you get an opening to move your conversation to the DMs. The Instagram version is to find people commenting on posts in your niche and commenting on their posts until you have an opening to take the conversation to DMs. Again, it can work amazingly well, but be in integrity with this approach; it is always about relationship first.

One place to look for inspiration (and to heal shadows) is the gate and line of your Unconscious Moon. In Gene Keys, it is the Attraction Sphere. It can give you some insight into the qualities, values, and type of content that will attract your people and help build a relationship with them. It can also show you where you might need to do some healing work so that you can attract people from a clear frequency. Also, conscious sun gate because it's your strongest energy.

. . .

Momentum is an essential part in attracting customers. You have your own energy and momentum, but your community and content will also create and add to it. In my opinion, this explains why the big names can do pretty much anything where advertising is concerned. They have created sufficient momentum, and their community gives them authority, adding different pieces of energy to the content, making it more appealing to a broader audience.

Building an audience becomes much easier the more people you have in your community. Once people are in your community, you can sell to them. You attract people by holding your frequency by speaking your truth loud and proud, and customers come to you. That's the secret. But, if you look for ways to amplify your momentum, that's how you get quantum results. It's about combining energy AND strategy.

MONEY IN YOUR BUSINESS

NO MATTER YOUR ENERGY TYPE, you will want to have some safety structures built-in. In her book Big Magic (which should be required reading for anyone wanting to earn money off their creativity), Elizabeth Gilbert says that you need to treat your (creative project of whatever type) like a baby. You need to let it grow and learn and figure itself out before you expect it to pay the bills.

I know this is counter to what you hear all over the internet: people go from nothing to 6 figures in a month. While that can happen, it's not typical, and if you're expecting your income from a new business to support you right out of the gate, it's going to put a lot of pressure on you and your creation. Do you work well under pressure? Do you love what you're doing when you're under pressure? Maybe you do, but for me, that's not the case. Diversifying your income streams is one of the best ways to create stability so that you can get your business off the ground and get through your low ebbs in energy without being stressed out or feeling like you have to do something to bring money in. Just a little disclaimer, I'm not a financial advisor and don't claim to be. Make aligned

decisions about your money, and get the right professional advice. The discussion below is food for thought.

1. **Semi-passive income:** Your money is where your energy is, so "passive income" is a bit of a misnomer. You will always have to feed energy into passive income projects at times. For Manifestors, once your energy has moved onto another creative project, the old one might feel a little flat. Once you have one product profitable, consider hiring someone to maintain it or selling it off to someone who will keep it going. You could also consider re-packaging content you have already created as bonuses in your new ventures. When you re-purpose content, make sure the product aligns with your current message. Something else to consider is packaging some of your older stuff (or creating something especially for the purpose) into upsells, downsells, offer bumps, etc. If you are trying to create passive income, remember that it will take maintenance, whether from your energy or someone else's.

2. **Affiliate Marketing:** This can take a lot of work, but the way I recommend it is that you have a few products that you recommend to your audience with affiliate links. Make them part of your existing customer journey, and you can capture some profit by piggybacking on your current marketing structures. You could also consider affiliate marketing on a larger scale, for example. You sell the course or whatever it is, and someone else fulfills it. I'm sure you've seen this with the big names. If you're good at attracting people to your message but don't feel like it's the right thing to offer a signature program, this could be a good option for you. With Manifestor energy, this could be an amazing way to structure your whole business model.

3. **Investments**: Find an advisor you jive with, and let their energy manage it. One of the best financial lessons is the power of compound interest. Set a regular withdrawal, and forget about it, even if it's a small amount. Don't watch and worry about it all the

time. You access it later, and it will need time to grow. Unlike property, this type of investment is usually liquid unless the fund is locked for some reason, usually tax reasons. Your advisor should help you figure out your risk tolerance and choose an investment right for you.

4. **Income property:** Property has its own energy. So do renters. If this is an option for you, think about the logistics of the property you purchase. Are you OK with the occasional sounds, smells, and sharing of outdoor space of renting out a basement apartment? Suppose you don't live at the property. Are you willing to hire someone to manage it or be available yourself for the emergencies and maintenance that come up, usually at inconvenient times? You can rent rooms or suites via Airbnb or similar sites to earn cash and not have the long-term renter situation, but then the turnover presents another thing to manage. Another way property can make you money is by living in a place long enough to give you equity. You only access equity when you sell your home but typically re-invest it in another place to live. Equity isn't really the type of money you can rely on to provide stability unless you're willing to sell your property.

Managing your money is an integral part of business. Reducing the emotional reactivity around it is typically the first and most important step. The majority of what I do is help people manage the emotional roller coaster of business in my small group and 1:1 containers. Find out more here: **http://carmenfarrellknapp.com/workwithme**. You also want to think of ways to use your money to serve and support you rather than being at its mercy.

Signing off and a few CTA's

I have other books in this series that are the bomb once you consistently use your strategy and authority. The logical next step is the book in this series, "Finding your Business Mojo with Human Design." This is where I really dive into leveraging your unique energy in your messaging and marketing. For example, where to look in your chart on who you might be best positioned to serve, how you best communicate, and how to use it to create your messaging.

Obvi, you can find me on social media. Handles change, but my name won't, so you can search me out as Carmen Farrell Knapp. I would love to hang out with you in the online world. Let me know how you're using Human Design in your business.

BOOK THREE

PROJECTORS

NO DEFINED SACRAL CENTER, NO MOTOR CENTER
CONNECTED TO THE THROAT CENTRE

Projectors

STRATEGY — Wait for an Invitation

NOT SELF THEME — Bitterness

SELF THEME — Success

Projectors usually know what to do and how. They tend to be systems queens and can implement and adjust a process to be beautifully functional and efficient. Under the best circumstances, you are working with people who see this and invite you for input and implement it. Projectors help others guide their energy, and it's how they get the name of "ultimate guide."

Ra Uru Hu (founder of human design) said that Projectors aren't here to work. While this may be true, it's such a loaded statement. Can I suggest an edit? The work of Projectors is different from that of Generators and Manifestors. It's more subtle, behind the scenes, and about developing relationships with others who are here to "work" (Ahem, Generators.) You will do what you can with the energy you have available to you, but most of the time, your "work" is getting Generators on board and helping them stick to it until completion.

INTRODUCTION TO BEING A PROJECTOR

ONE THING you are exceptionally well equipped to do is to help sacral beings direct their substantial life force energy towards actually completing stuff without getting distracted. Generators are known to be quitters, and if you can help them stop that, you will have more clients than you can ever help on your own. If that doesn't sound like "work," I don't know what is!

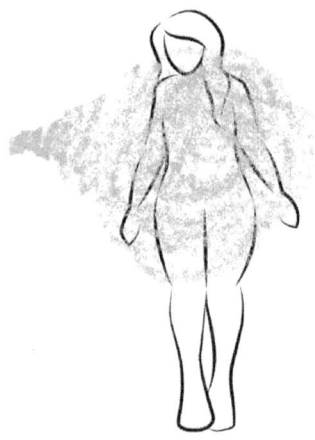

| *The Aura of a Projector*

The term Projector refers to a projected energy field. Your aura will penetrate others' g-center (identity center.) If you're recognized and invited into their world, this is fine. It can feel very invasive if you haven't had an invitation, even if your intentions are good. Part of your process is to know the other. You learn who you are by sampling the experiences of others and making sense of it. You use that information to inform your own choices and guide others.

Of all the energy types, Projectors have the most variation. There are many types of Projectors with different energetic ways of being, so it's hard to make generalizations about Projectors. Especially when you consider that energy type is just one layer of your energy, an essential layer because it is how others generally perceive you (whether they know it or not) and how you best make decisions.

Any profiling tool should empower you to create your own identity, not tell you what it means or who you are. That's your job as someone trying to develop themselves. Nowhere in human design says that Projectors can't work more than 3 hours a day. Someone has interpreted their design and made it mean something for them, and it seems to have caught on. When creating meaning from your chart, make sure it serves you, and know that you can change it. Human design is just a tool; it does not give you an identity. Any coach should have tools that provide context and guide you through creating meaning for yourself, not telling you what to do or think and who to be.

I think Projectors are most venerable to some of the dis-empowering stories circulating about what it means to be a Projector. I have a theory about this. Projectors can have very few centers defined. This will mean a lot of hanging gates in their chart. These gates in undefined centers do not meet another gate and create a channel. Energetically, these gates will always be searching to find people that complete the channel and activate the center. If you are a non-energy Projector around someone with a defined motor, you will pick up on that energy and be able to use it while you're in their aura, which might be a little bit of an addiction if you feel you have to produce like a Generator. You can also pick up conditioning in these undefined gates and centers.

As a Projector, you can have as few as two centers defined (and as many as 8, but that would be rare indeed.) Where you have definition is your own, consistent energy. It will be familiar to you. The energy you pick up from those around you comes and goes and isn't *actually* yours, but you have access to it sometimes. Here's where my theory begins. Unless you know about this mechanism of picking up on the energy of those around you, you will just assume everything you experience is your energy. You might not know why, but you will naturally attract people who complete your channels or give you a little energy hit. You also live in a Generator world that always has access to the sacral motor and doesn't understand others who don't. This creates a culture of going and doing that may not match your energy. You might even go so far as to create meaning about this, possibly labeling yourself as lazy? Unable? Bad at marketing/business/making money/whatever?

Now, add the Projector's need to be recognized and invited to this situation. This (in my opinion) creates the perfect setup for people-pleasing as you try to fill the need to be recognized and get a little extra energy; just a lonely Projector trying to keep up in this Generator world. You might assume that Reflectors have it worse, but they seem to know when energy isn't theirs, as well as an aura that naturally repels others' energy. So they kind of sidestep thewhole question of "is this energy mine?" because it never is. Plus, they are less venerable to picking up conditioning from the people around them and more susceptible to conditioning from the energetic environment.

Any energy type with three or fewer centers defined seems to have this problem of being a pseudo Reflector and confusion around what is theirs. Pseudo Reflector is NOT a human design term; it's just one I use to describe this situation of having little definition, picking up on the energy of/conditioning from those around you, and not always knowing how to manage it.

Let's get back to the Projector types. You can start by categorizing Projectors into energy Projectors and non-energy Projectors. If you have one or more of the "motors" defined, you are an energy Projector, which means that you will have consistent energy from the solar plexus, root, or ego center to supply you with the power to do the things you need and want to do. When you think of the typical description of a Projector, you probably hear about a non-energy Projector; the wise nap queens who work 3 hours a day. While that may be true and possible for you, it doesn't mean you don't or can't work like the best of them to accomplish what you want. In any business, there will be seasons where some divine hustle will be necessary.

A "Classic Projector" is a non-energy Projector (no motors defined) and neither of the pressure centers defined (root or head.) Definition is only below the throat, meaning g-center and spleen. As its name suggests, people typically describe this when talking about Projectors—laid back, low energy, super wise guides.

A "Mental Projector" has 2 or 3 of the top energy centers defined (Head, Anja and/or Throat.) Because you have a lot of mental energy, you tend to be a deep thinker and will probably be good at conceptualizing complex ideas into systems and processes. Your authority type will be "environmental" or "no inner authority." Don't get confused with no authority. That's just crazy talk.

Another way of describing Projectors is by authority. Emotional Projectors are an energy-type Projector who will need to feel their way to a decision through their emotional wave. This center will also provide consistent motor energy. Splenic Projectors have the only authority available to Projectors that doesn't require some form of waiting or processing time after an invitation. Self-projected Projectors have G center authority connected to the throat and no motors connected to the throat. They have to speak their truth and talk out decisions with someone they trust. Ego projected Projectors have the heart center connected to the g-center and follow their heart to its desires. Finally, mental Projectors, described in the previous paragraph, remember the brainy ones? This is a whopping five possibilities out of the seven possible authority types.

. . .

All Projector types are good at guiding the energy of others. They are often called wise, and most of the time, their energy is both soothing and stimulating to be around. Generators (particularly Manifesting Generators) and Projectors seem to magnetize towards each other. I believe that you can help them utilize their sacral energy without ruffling their feathers like a Manifestor or Reflector often can. Plus, they give you that little boost of sacral energy, which is nice.

Strategy: Wait to be recognized and invited

I'm going to tell you a familiar story. My good (Projector) friend was in a wedding party. She was the odd one out because the other two bridesmaids were friends, and she was the sister-in-law. The maid of honor kept taking on all the organizing tasks leading up to the wedding. She didn't listen to what the bride wanted and made a colossal muck of organizing the shower and bachelorette. My friend, reading between the lines, and noticing the bride's mounting anxiety, wanted to try to jump in and help fix things. Which, of course, she got the energetic equivalent of the middle finger for her efforts.

We were walking our pups on the beach as she was venting her bitterness about this. She knew she could organize things to reduce stress on the bride. I knew that too because she is the friend who will go to the ends of the earth to make it perfect for you. She's the one who knows what you want, even if you don't. After about 40 minutes of talking, I was like, "Girl, can I step into coach mode for a minute?" I asked her what she was making it all mean. After a little digging, she said (I'm paraphrasing and maybe exaggerating for the sake of the story) that the wedding would be ruined. The bride, already had it bad enough with a covid wedding, would look back on the experience with regret, and that it would be my friend's fault because she could have made it better.

. . .

She tried to help without being recognized; it kept ending in bitterness. I asked her what she *was* being invited to do in her role as a bridesmaid. Her role was to show up in a pretty dress and have fun. All the rest was not her circus, not her monkeys. In short, it wasn't her responsibility to take on and personalize the results. But, if it was interfering with her ability to enjoy the wedding, that *was* on her to manage. Before returning to friend mode, my final question was: What do you need to change in your thinking/who do you need to show up as so that relationships aren't strained after the fact, and you can enjoy yourself at this wedding. Once she let go of her need to change the results and make them hers, she had a great time at the wedding.

I see variations on this story all the time with Projectors. In your business, this can show up as changing niche frequently, trying to pursue people or situations to force a result. Scope creep is a huge problem (serving people outside of your scope because you want to please them and they invited and recognized you, so you said yes.)

You are also prone to be taken advantage of by customers because of poor ground rules and boundaries. While none of these are exclusive to Projectors, the mechanism of wanting to be recognized and trying to push yourself into an invitation is pure Projector. It amplifies you trying to *be* someone or something you're not so that you can be recognized.

As a Projector entrepreneur, you want to invest your energy in becoming known for one thing. Nicheing is your best friend in business because your secret marketing sauce will attract people to you by establishing yourself as an expert. Sticking with one thing means you will utilize your energy to build your reputation as the expert in that one thing, rather than spreading it out among multiple things or always starting from scratch. People are drawn to your solution and YOU because you are authentic, passionate, and know your stuff. That's how you have to show up for people to notice and recognize you as the genius you are with the solution to their problem. The invitations to work together will follow shortly after.

Some things to consider as a Projector:

- You're going to operate best by staying in your own lane until someone asks you for your opinion or help
- Notice if you are reaching or pushing for a particular outcome. That's Manifestor territory and will lead you to bitterness
- Not all invitations are made equal. Sometimes saying yes to one kind of meh invitation will tie you up, so you can't say yes to the invitation that is a hell yes.
- Use your energy wisely on invitations that are an 80% + match for you. Your authority is your guide on which invitations to say yes to. This means developing the skill of saying no. Yes, it can be a complete sentence.
- Nothing will drain your energy quicker than pursuing invitations that are not forthcoming for you. Plus, it will distract you from the invitations available to you at the moment.
- Notice if you are trying to take responsibility for results that aren't yours/you haven't been invited to consult on. Not everything is yours to fix, even though we both know you know how to do it better
- Generators are going to do what Generators are going to do. If they're smart, they will ask you for your help. If not, let them screw it up on their own. Get good at saying not mine. Maybe they somehow pull it out of the bag with a win. It's still not yours.

AUTHORITY FOR PROJECTORS

AUTHORITY IS DETERMINED BY THE CENTER(S) YOU HAVE
DEFINED

AUTHORITY FOR PROJECTORS

EMOTIONAL AUTHORITY (51% of the population)

This is the most common authority. About 50% of the population have emotional authority. While it is common, most people are unaware of how to use emotional information and fuel that a defined solar plexus can give you. It is an awareness center for emotional processing and one of the 4 "motors" in the body graph. Using this authority takes time to process emotions, and you guessed it, awareness of the highs and lows of the wave.

Emotional authority is NOT figuring out how you feel about a decision and making decisions based on emotion.

It is about using the different emotions of your emotional wave as information to come to clarity. You feel your way through the highs and lows of emotion about that decision until you just know what the right path is.

You are an energy Projector if you have emotional authority. Meaning you have (at least) one "motor" defined, giving you more consistent energy than other Projectors. Learning to leverage this energy will be important to do "the things." But, it isn't inexhaustible. You will want to schedule time for yourself away from others to rest. Learn when enough is enough, and don't push beyond what you have energy for.

The emotional wave is a mechanical process. You will have a stimulus that you respond to that triggers an emotion that you follow through the high, low, and in between. This isn't avoidable. You will have an emotional wave regardless. You can suppress or enhance emotion, but it happens whether you want to experience it or not. The best-case scenario is that you learn to use emotion as the experience and tool it is meant to be for you and then allow it to flow through you. They can get stuck when you try to repress emotions, creating an elongated wave. Part of your routine should be to feel the emotions of that moment and see if you can feel where you are resisting emotion. Allow yourself to feel in a safe space if there are unresolved emotions.

The thing with emotion is that your mind and ego will want to get involved and label it as good or bad, this or that, and you will start to create stories around the emotional experience. Ego wants to move you out of discomfort as quickly as possible, but much of your growth as an entrepreneur will come from your superpower of being able to ride out the wave of discomfort. If you can learn not to identify with your emotions and mine the truth they have to tell you, then you will be unstoppable! Much of this work is awareness about what you make your emotions mean and allowing them to flow without creating resistance.

. . .

The key with the emotional wave is to make sure you have come to neutral before deciding. Does this mean you need to ride out the emotional wave on every decision? NO! But be aware of when you feel triggered (high or low) and wait until you have more emotional clarity. Most people can understand not deciding a low part of the wave, but it's equally important to avoid the high state. Think of a time when you've been super excited about something. You commit on the spot and find that after, when you aren't on the top of the wave, you don't actually have the energy, or it is something that you aren't that passionate about, but… you said yes and are stuck seeing it through.

Depending on which channel(s) are defined will give your wave a different flavor. You may have multiple channels defined, and you can experience the wave differently. The type of wave will also determine what invitations your energy is available for. Decisions of this nature will be important to give yourself the time to process and ride out the wave, as these are the types of decisions that will have the most power for you. Not every invitation you respond to is super important, but the things that are hardwired for you to respond to are determined by the active channels in your authority. When you look at which channels are creating your emotional wave, you can also look up information on the circuitry it belongs to and the channel and gates to get a better picture of what you will respond to.

While your strategy is to wait for an invitation, your authority will tell you if you have the energy available for it. Unlike a splenic authority with a clear yes or no, you will rarely be 100% sure because you have to feel out the decision through the high and low and everything in between your emotional wave. So for you, pretty sure is good enough. Be aware of when your mind starts to try to sway you one way or another. Stick with the feeling you get from a decision, not the thoughts, stories, and drama.

The solar plexus is an awareness center for emotional energy. You will experience emotional energy in a specific, defined way. It will be unique to you but reliable, consistent, and predictable. You will seek things out that give you an emotional experience because this is part of how you meet the world, learn, and grow. If you have this center defined, you are here to live a robust, vibrant, and varied emotional life. Your inner authority will respond to the experiences, relationships, and things that let you play out the emotional experience. But, your emotional wave won't respond to *every* invitation.

The type of circuitry will give you a clue as to what you are hardwired to respond to in life (see the types of waves for more on that specifically.) But, your authority will give you a yes or a no, not a why. Your mind and ego will not be satisfied. So, there is a practice of quieting the mind when following your authority.

Your emotions are meant to enhance your life and use the energy of emotion to create. Most of us are socialized to view emotion as something to be restrained, resisted, or, worst case, be ashamed of. So it can be a completely new concept to some to allow emotion to have the deciding vote in how you do life. The first step is to start to become aware of your emotions. Notice if a specific emotion signals the start of your wave. Observe how you move through your wave with different triggers. Start to develop your vocabulary on your emotions, and notice the nuances between similar emotions.

. . .

Journaling can help with this. Another technique is to check in with yourself at each meal, morning and night, and notice what you feel. The more awareness you bring to your emotions, the better you will understand how to work with this powerful energy.

Here are a few things to keep in mind when working with emotional energy:

- An emotion is just a vibration in the body. Some of the more intense emotional energy like anxiety, or even excitement, will pass through you. The chemical spike an emotion creates in your blood lasts approximately 90 seconds. So, if you can stay with the feeling, observing yourself and breathing through it, it will flow through you. If you resist or fight emotion, that spike can extend, or worse, rebound with more intensity.
- Most of working with emotional energy is learning not to resist. Allow it to flow, observe how you feel through the whole experience, come to neutral, then act. Resistance can cause your emotional energy to get stuck, and this is how you can potentially experience extended times in lower vibration emotions like depression.
- Avoid labeling emotions as positive or negative. The energy of emotion is neutral until you assign meaning to it with thoughts. You are designed to experience the whole range of emotions, not just the "positive" ones. Taking the mindset of observing the sensation of emotion in your body will help.

When you are around people without definition in the solar plexus, they will pick up on your emotional wave (whether they know it or not!) and amplify it back to you. While you can share your emotions with others, your emotional wave is yours, and if you are trying to work through something, it is best to do it out of the energy of others.

Types of Emotional Wave

The Source of all Waves: Solar Plexus to Sacral: 6-59: Channel of Intimacy

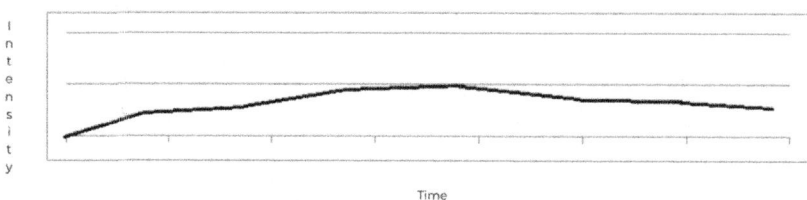

Solar Plexus to Sacral Center: 6-59 Channel of Intimacy

The source of all waves is about the intimacy in relationships that allows people to create something new. It will respond to relationships that can lead to the creativity to build or create. The channel is called the channel of mating, or intimacy, and can refer to creating new life or any other creative process between 2 people. This wave responds to the things that create a connection between people. It will flow up then plateau with each connection. It is a gentle rise, plateau, then drift back down. The theme is about human connection, responding to relationships, and seeking out the connections that will lead to something new. It is a reasonably gentle wave and very good at relating to others. Anyone with this channel will be a Generator and will want to follow the relationships that lead them to create things they are passionate about.

Tribal Wave: Solar Plexus to Root: 49-19: Channel of Synthesis and Solar Plexus to Heart: 37-40: Channel of Community

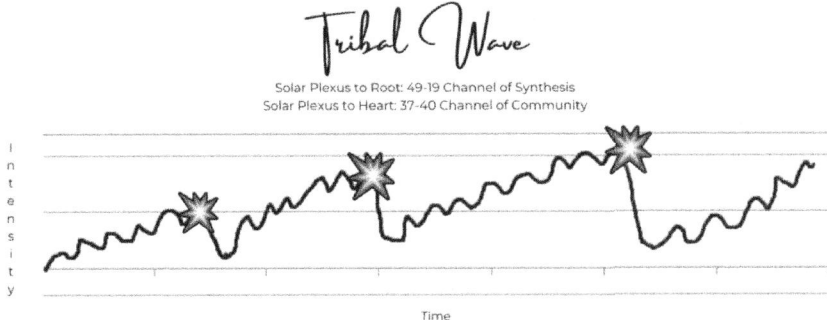

The tribal wave will respond to survival or need in the intimate community. It is part of the tribal circuitry. It responds to the needs of the tribe or family (tribal is different from collective, which is concerned with the greater good, tribal is concerned with the survival and thriving of people in the close circle.) It is concerned with resources and providing the tools you and your tribe need to survive. Physical connection is a key component to this wave, and when you are triggered, it will help you ground yourself to connect physically. It operates like a ratchet. You are triggered, then relax back, kind of like you shake it off. It may take a few times before you reach the explosion point, but you will eventually get agitated enough by the trigger to have a release of emotion. Then there will be a reset. This wave is not subtle and can feel a bit out of control at times. Knowing how this wave operates and your typical responses will help you find positive ways to release the emotional energy. Do you pick a fight so that you can hug it out? Perhaps it would be easier to ask for a hug. Just sayin'

. . .

The Individual Wave: Solar Plexus to Root: 55-39:Channel of Emoting, Solar Plexus to Throat 22-12: Channel of Openness

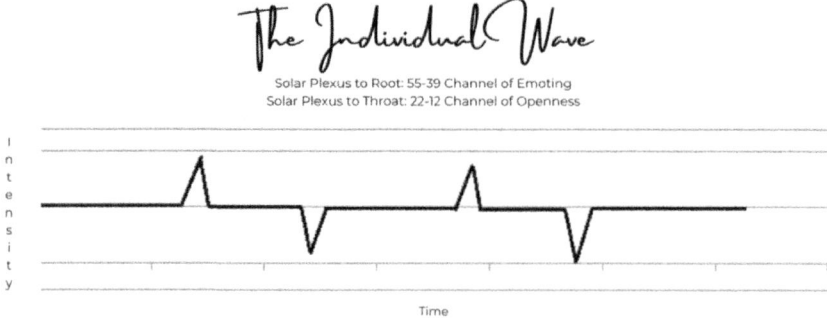

Solar Plexus to Root: 55-39 Channel of Emoting
Solar Plexus to Throat: 22-12 Channel of Openness

The individual wave is characterized by passion, and your mood is the expression of this wave. It can be a wavy wave. At times you will want to share this emotion with others, and at times it is best kept just for your experience alone. It has peaks then comes back to steadiness, then it drops, then comes back to steady. You want to be conscious of when you need time alone to feel your emotions without the influence of others. This will help you avoid getting trapped in the lows and keep moving with the mood. It is important to allow yourself space, connect to your needs and desires, and learn to ground yourself when it gets a little too wavy. The channels of this wave are part of the individual circuitry and will respond to the things that help you grow and advance as an individual.

The Abstract Wave: Solar Plexus to Root: 30-41: Channel of Recognition, Solar Plexus to Throat: 36-35: Chanel of Transitoriness

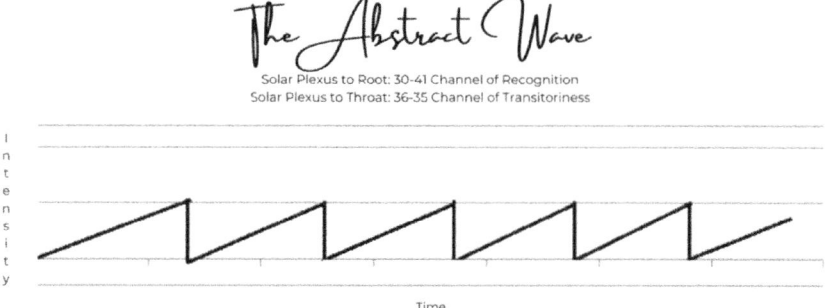

There will be a gentler rhythm to this wave than the individual wave. It will ebb and flow by responding to experience. The two channels associated with this wave carry a great deal of friction. The 35-36 seeks new beginnings and wants to respond to the invitations worth pursuing. The 30-41 communicate the lessons learned through overcoming friction through emotion. Remember that this is your natural energetic state, so following strategy and authority and allowing this wave to operate as it is meant will help you determine the worthwhile conflict and hold the vision and optimism that each experience brings. This wave can present challenges when you enter into an experience with an expectation that is not met, causing an emotional crash. It is important not to attach yourself to an outcome; Rather, you are going into an experience for the sake of the emotion it will create and the things you can learn from it.

Splenic Authority (9 % of the population)

The spleen is all about intuition, survival, and the physical body. Intuition can have many voices, and getting to know the communication from your authority is key. You might even have conditioning around "intuition" and what it means to be intuitive. As the Spleen is responsible for survival (both as an individual and of the tribe), you will be sensitive to situations that trigger your spidy sense about how viable, healthy or beneficial something is for you or the community.

The typical description of splenic authority is that you have an inner knowing of what is right or wrong for you. Oh yeah, that makes it totally clear (that was sarcasm in case the written word failed to communicate the nuance.) Welcome to life with a splenic authority. There is a physical sensation to this "knowing." But, it can be subtle, and the splenic authority will only answer once, so if you're not paying attention at that moment, you can miss the cue.

For you, more than any other authority type, you will need to find ways to stay present in the moment and grounded in your body. Your mind will try to override the splenic decisions by using logic. Remember the role of the mind as an external authority. Getting out of your head and into your body is the only way to hear the intuitive hit of the spleen. Many splenic authorities will find meditation or another form of grounding and centering practice helpful to tune into the physical sensations. It also gives you space to observe thoughts and the tricky ways they manipulate your decisions.

You want to feel the difference between mind/thought/ego energy and your splenic intuition. Eckhart Tolle's "The Power of Now" is a compelling book for you, and I strongly recommend reading it. Several times.

. . .

I will attempt to make concrete sense of the splenic center for you. Each of the gates of the spleen has its own flavor or sensation. Some of the gates will have a physical sensation, and all of them have a fundamental fear associated with it. I like to flip the narrative about the fear gates of the spleen and choose to think of them as indicators of the things your energy is available for.

They create a theme in your life that gives you purpose and can reveal some of your core values. For example, gate 18's association is fear of authority. This might indicate that you value freedom or have a purpose of questioning or challenging authority. It also might be a theme in your life to overcome your fear of power and something you can help others do. I want to let you decide what they mean to you, but I hope you lean into creating meaning that supports you.

I'm going to run through the gates of the spleen and what some of the connections are. Look at where you have definition in the spleen, and which one(s) create channels. I've included the shadow and gifts of these gates, taken from Richard Rudd's Gene Keys, so you can use it as a litmus test of how you are expressing the energy. Ideally, you want to express the high-frequency energy of the gate rather than indulging fear. If the gate is linked to one of the senses, I have also included it. This may help you zero in on how your spleen communicates.

Gate 18: Fear of Authority.

Shadow: Victim mindset- All judgment is self-judgment, and the level you identify with your judgments is the degree of resistance you will create.

Gift: Integrity: You have a knack for testing the integrity of people and your environment to determine what needs to evolve.

Physical sensation: Touch. You can determine the physical strength of structures at a vibrational level. There may be a tactile element to your splenic communication.

Gate 28: Fear of Death

Shadow: Purposelessness (fear that you will die without finding your purpose)

Gift: Totality (Trust in the process of life, *despite* fear)

Physical sensation: Sound vibration. Your inner knowing may have an auditory quality to it eg, ringing in the ears or hearing your guidance as voices or conversations. You may hear phrases or conversations, or other noises as your spleen tries to communicate. Watch for patterns in your inner dialogue.

Gate 32: Fear of Failure

Shadow: Failure (Seeing learning as failure) This also has roots in the collective fear for survival as a species. The fear of being ostracized from the group literally meant death. There is an element of social fear expressed in this gate. Translated into modern times, survival = money for many people

Gift: Preservation (knowing what is worth preserving and what can be let go to evolve) Also, very good at sensing which relationships will lead to growth.

Sensation: Breath/breathing. This gate is about support and survival, and breath is the most fundamental resource for survival. Observe your breath when you are listening to your splenic authority. If you hold your breath or speed up, it may give you clues.

Gate 44: Fear of the Past

Shadow: Interference (this is an abstract one, but I like to think of it as clearing out the karma, patterns, and programming interfering with expressing ourselves at a high frequency.)

Gift: Teamwork

Sensation: Sense of smell. You can smell the people, situations, and destiny right for you. You are a genius at reading people. You will probably instinctually know who's invitations feel right for you.

Gate 48: Fear of inadequacy

Shadow: Inadequacy (this is the root of all fears, and shadow that we are inherently inadequate)

Gift: Resourcefulness

Sensation: You can "see" the answer through the darkness. Your spleen may communicate with flashes or insights in a visual way. Notice what draws you and what aesthetically appeals.

Gate 50: Fear of responsibility

Shadow: Corruption (This can refer to political and social corruption, but it also refers to how energetic expression can be corrupted by fear, ego, and the mind that restricts evolution and growth.)

Gift: Equilibrium (Sense of balance and cosmic order to the world)

Sensation: While not a physical sensation per sea, those with this gate have a sense of equilibrium or balance. It may be that you have a feel for when something is "off."

Gate 57 Fear of the Future

Shadow: Unease (pervasive sense that something terrible is coming, pessimism)

Gift: Intuition

Sensation: Hearing. You have a sense of interpreting what people are really saying. You can hear the nuances in sound that others may not be as sensitive to.

Ego Projected Authority (most rare with less than 0.5% of the population)

Hey, there rare one! It is a pretty unusual situation you got going on with your energy. You're even rarer than **Reflector**s. You have two centers and one channel defined. That leaves a whole lot of hanging gates in undefined centers whose energy is only available to you when that center is activated by someone in your aura or the transits. You will probably find that you seek those who complete channels for you and bring definition to your chart (we all do this, it's not just you, but most people have more of their own defined energy.)

When you have external energy activating channels to centers that would give you another authority, it will provide you with the sense that you should use that authority to make decisions. This is called a conditioned inner authority. That isn't going to lead to good things for you.

· · ·

The channel you have is the Channel of Initiation. This means you want to be first and may be a little bit… competitive? The great part of this channel (especially for Projectors who are here to guide the energy of others) is your ability to recognize the potential for transformation in others. But this channel, especially as one of the stronger energies in your body, will give you an urge to initiate like a Manifestor. Waiting to be recognized and invited is the only way to enter a decision for you, so get wise to when you want to initiate.

The two centers you have defined will also give you clues to what invitations your energy will respond to. The G center (love and direction) and the Heart center (will.) For example, Gate 25 in the G center is about loving all living things without discrimination. That's some powerful love energy. Look at the other gates activated in your defined centers for clues to which invitations lead you to express your energy in that way. Being a Projector who is here to know others is a bit of a paradox. Your energy needs others to express itself, while your definition is in the two centers that primarily drive individual energy. Bringing harmony to the self/other question will probably be a theme for you.

G-center Love Gates

Gate

10 Love of Self

15 Love of Humanity (even in the extreme expression)

25 Love of all living things without discrimination

46 Love of the Body

· · ·

G-center Direction Gates

These are like perspective points, and they will influence what decisions will be best for you. These gates are also called role gates and can give you clues about how you are meant to express your purpose.

Gate

1 Choosing a direction in the present moment

2 The driver. You can see all directions and stay grounded in the now

7 Looking forward to make decisions. A planner and master of delayed gratification

13 Looking back to make decisions. What has worked in the past? What needs change?

Heart Center Gates

Gate

21 To be in control, to control circumstances

26 To be the best, to excel, to refine

40 To deliver, to provide at a material level

51 To be competitive, to be first

It will be vital for you to know how your inner authority speaks to you and learn how to sort out when you are drifting towards making not-self decisions. Part of your process is to talk it out with people to figure out what is right for you. What you are trying to determine with these conversations is what do you *want?*

. . .

Your desires are the guideposts for you. I can already hear the conditioning coming up around "selfishness." Notice that as the BS it is. You set your own direction in life, not follow others. Your desires are what will lead you in the right direction. The conversations you have are a sounding board to help you understand your desires.

Like all authorities that need to speak it out, it's important to have people in your life who are good at listening, holding up the mirror for you, and not giving advice until asked. If you don't have anyone else around, you can talk to yourself, the dog, plants, whatever. You want to actually express it as sound so you can listen to your voice. Journaling is another way to get your thoughts out of your head so you can see what you are really trying to say.

Self Projected Authority (2.5% of the population)

Hey beautiful human. You have a clear identity and express it through the voice. To have this authority, you have (at least) one of 4 channels that connect the G-center with the throat. As someone who has an incarnation cross of the Vessel of Love, I can't think of a more beautiful and efficient energetic way to express the spectrum of individuality. But, like the Ego authority, you have a bit of a paradox between your energy type (relies on invitations to guide the energy of others) and a very personal expression of self.

Your voice is a powerful tool. You must speak your truth. To express your truth, you have to know your truth. Reflecting on what is true for you is super important. What have you always known to be true? What feels the most "like you?" Human Design can be a fantastic way to feel out what is true for your energy. You are a seeker of truth, and you help others find their truth. Your authority will seek to answer the question: What is true?

You are also going to have a fixed direction in life and are not meant to follow the direction of others. You can sample it, and if it is true for you, by all means, go that way. If not, decline that invitation. In my observations, many Projectors forget that they can R.S.V.P. no. (See my earlier rant about people-pleasing.)

The type of circuitry that your channel(s) belongs to will tell you a lot about what your energy is available to be invited into. Collective circuitry is about contributing to the growth of the whole in an impersonal way. You contribute your knowledge and peace out. You don't stick around to see what the collective does with it. Individual circuitry is about empowering others by being an example. You change yourself and show others it is possible. Integration circuitry is about how your individual expression impacts others. None of the channels from the G-center to the throat are tribal, which is about community and support.

Channel

7-31 Channel of the Alpha

Collective Circuit: Leadership through logic. Advisors to leaders

13-33 Channel of the Prodigal

Collective Circuit. Understanding of the past that informs future decisions. Reflection that contributes to the greater good

. . .

1-8 Channel of Inspiration

Individual Circuit. Empower others to live their truth by living yours

10-20 Channel of Awakening

Integration Circuit. Commitment to transform on an individual level to inspire others to do the same

Like all authorities that need to speak it out, it's essential to have people in your life who are good at listening, holding up the mirror for you, and not giving advice until asked. If you don't have anyone else around, you can talk to yourself, the dog, plants, whatever. You want to actually express it as sound so you can listen to your voice. Journaling is another way to get your thoughts out of your head so you can see what you are really trying to say.

Environmental/No Inner Authority (2% of the population)

As one of the types whose authority depends on talking it out, you might benefit from reading the previous descriptions of authority as there may be some nuggets you resonate with. My take on environmental authority is different from anyone else I've heard speak about. I want you to think about what feels true for you in relation to your authority, as I've drawn some conclusions from my experience working with Human design, deep contemplation, and the traditional teachings on environmental authority. So, make sure you take what resonates and discard the rest, as I may have gone a little rogue. I sometimes feel bad for the energy types and authorities that aren't as common. Information can be hard to come by, and when I wrote this, I intended to give you as much as I give the Generators.

· · ·

If you have this authority, you are a mental Projector. Your gift is to read the potential of energy. In your case, you get an invitation and need to assess whether it is right for you by feeling out its viability with your energy field. You don't have any centers defined below the throat, meaning your natural energy is very mental, conceptual, and logical. This presents a bit of a conundrum as your thoughts will never drive your inner authority or decisions. Any energy in your physical body will be inconsistent and often not even yours. The whole point of listening to your authority is to hear your soul's guidance.

The soul communicates through the body, not the mind. I'm sure you're connecting the dots, my brainy one, and coming up with the conclusion of how the heck am I supposed to do this authority thing if I can't use my mental energy. You will need to get out of your head and into your body and environment to get the direction you need.

Deep breaths, my friend, let's break it down. A centering practice is going to be very helpful for you to be able to get a feel for your physical body. Many times people with this authority (or just people with head and Ajna definition, in general, find meditation difficult. The mind keeps getting its sticky little fingers all over your meditation practice and distracting you from being in the body. Using a mantra will give your mind something to focus on while you get on with your centering practice. Transcendental Meditation is something many mental Projectors find beneficial to feel grounded in their physical body and get used to how their body feels at different times. In short, it helps you practice feeling what energy is "self" and what is "not-self."

There are two things you will need to get clarity on to use your authority: How you feel in your body about a decision, and what is your energy/truth and what isn't. Learning how to ground yourself in the physical body will help reduce some of the static or interference your very active mind will try to throw off. Now that you have some awareness of what you're feeling in the physical body, you need to talk it out with a few people. In this way, you essentially run the energy through you and their combined energy, and in this process, you can figure out what is yours and what isn't. What feels right for you, and decide whether you take up the invitation or not.

Talking it out helps you dissect the thoughts and feelings you have on a situation. In a way, it is similar to an emotional authority where they need to feel out their emotions through a period of time to come to enough emotional clarity to make a decision. You need to process the energy through your aura and the auras of others to come to physical clarity. In the end, you will just know what is right for you. If you don't, talk it out a bit more.

It is pretty important who you use as your sounding board because they will, without meaning to, project their energy onto you. It is the nature of having so many open centers to draw this kind of energy, which is why your centering practice is so important. As you learn how different energy feels in your body, you can let the things, words, situations, and environments pass through you rather than bogging you down by holding on to it. What is left after you let the energy that is not for you go is the gold. The invitations will lead to miraculous places.

Journaling is another practice that will help you dissect the mental energy of a situation. The guiding thought or reflection is: How does this make me feel/is this energy for me or not.

You are a profound thinker. When you speak your truth, others get massive value from your insights. The other side of this is that you want recognition for your thinking. It is crucial to make sure you are waiting for others to invite you into the conversation because your wisdom will be unappreciated if you insert yourself into it. People have to be ready for you, and the ones that are will experience a huge expansion of their minds to be around you. Don't force, don't seek. They will come to you.

Signature: Success Not-Self Theme: Bitterness

Your signature is how you know you are on the right path. When you feel successful, you are following your strategy and making decisions from your authority. This is a good health check for your energy. If you are experiencing more Bitterness than Success, you want to look at how you are making decisions and where you might be operating from conditioning and/or not-self.

Success does not necessarily equal money or achieving a goal. It is the sensation of having used your energy successfully. For Projectors, this means you helped guide the energy of others towards success. The word success probably has associations for you that aren't quite what Ra was talking about when he identified this as your signature. Try borrowing the Generator signature of satisfaction and mixing it with your concept of success. Does that help you feel the vibration of success? It is a physical sensation in the body that you are looking for.

The feeling of success is also where your money is at. It means you are operating in alignment with your purpose, prosperity, and energy. Success is the vibration you emit to the universe to draw in all the incredible things in the world. This is how you know you have your vibration set to the right frequency, so follow the feeling of success in your life and business, and money will be there.

In my experience, your purpose and how you fulfil it is pretty damn successful. If you're curious about your purpose, check out the gates of your Incarnation Cross found in your conscious and unconscious sun and earth.

PROJECTOR GOALS

SUCCESS IS the goal of a Projector. Success is not about achieving an arbitrary number, although Projectors can benefit from setting measures of success. It is more about a feeling. How can you use your energy to feel success? What types of people do you want to work with to enhance your sense of success? What things lead to more bitterness? When was the last time you felt successful with your marketing? Messaging? Offers? Community? Do you feel like your business model leads to success? Do you like what you're doing? What parts of your work do you not like doing? These are important questions for a Projector to reflect on. They will give you some direction when you set goals.

Goals can be challenging for Projectors because you can set a narrow definition of success. If you aren't careful, the way you interpret failure can be discouraging. Failure is part of business. Not every endeavor is going to be successful. Bitterness over the failures can lead to some dark places and influence how you approach risk. Change and growth involve risk. For you, managing your interpretations of "failure" will be necessary.

Your success is going to rely on others. You can't control the actions (and invitations) of others. You want to keep clearing out the bitterness left behind when things and situations don't go as you planned. Think about what expectations you are applying to your goals beyond your control.

Consider setting a focus for each 90-day segment in your business (you might align to the quarters, but if you're going all rebel on me, set your 90 days whenever you want.) Decide what element of your business you want to grow in this time. Is it audience growth? Is it messaging alignment? Is it reach? Is it traffic to your sales page or webinar? Is it sales? Set a target on your 90-day goal, but realize that there will be some flexibility in that metric as you progress towards it and have more invitations to respond to. When you have more information, update your goals.

Leave enough flexibility in your goals to say yes to the invitations to the amazing things that come up. The problem with committing strongly to your goals in advance is that you lose your power of invitations that come up in the moment. This is especially important for splenic authority, an in-the-moment type of authority. Your authority will tell you if you have the energy to do something. Rigid goals will commit your energy in advance, leaving you tied up and unable to respond in the moment, or you find that you don't actually have energy for the things you committed to, which means set the goals. But they need to be tended to along the way.

FYI, I'm speaking as a Generator with a completely open will center, so you may have energy elsewhere in your chart that lets you do goals a little differently. In general, when you're setting goals, keep in mind that your power is in the moment, AND you need to have some direction in your business.

I guess you've been burned by the typical (heavy-handed?) advice on goals in the past and are a bit hesitant even to set them. You can only set so many goals and not reach them before you start telling yourself a story about your abilities to achieve and goal set. Be honest, have you given up on goals? My advice is to shift your mindset about goals. You want to have high-level navigational goals. I'm probably going to be hunted down by the SMART goal people, but leave them vague. They can be dreamy and fuzzy. One of my high-level goals is to have a business with a 2x/year launch for a signature program or mastermind and a few 1:1 clients. Traditional goal advice would want me to start filling in the details, give it a deadline and assign measurements of success. It's OK if you don't.

BUSINESS MODELS FOR PROJECTORS

BEING A NON-ENERGY TYPE, you will have to account for the inevitable highs and lows in your energy. Automation is your best friend. So is outsourcing. You want to think of ways to set your business up to make offers and accept people's money while you nap. Or, if you make your money in spurts, consider funnelling some of that money into investments that make passive or semi-passive income, where you can use your money to make more money. While you may not be on this planet to "work" like the Generators, you are here to be supported financially while you guide others. That doesn't just happen. I mean, it kind of does once you have some momentum, but usually, you have to make some good decisions on how you set your business up and feed the money generation machine with consistent Calls to Action for your customers.

It might be the Generator in me, but I've never found there to be a truly passive source of income. Meaning you need to inject some form of energy into it to keep it going and producing. So, let's say that your offer is a course. How are you directing traffic to that course? Are there links in your automated email sequences? Do you have social media posts that

CTA to your course? Do you run ads? Do you talk about your offer often enough for your followers to know you have one?

I listen to a podcast with a regular guest who is a Projector. She appeared for months before she mentioned her offer. She recommended her free stuff, but not her offer. I never went to check out the freebies, but when she mentioned the amazing course she was selling, I went to buy it right away. Imagine how many more people she might have been able to reach if she talked about it more!

Another Projector scenario: You've already met my friend in the last section (the bridesmaid.) She is a massage therapist who has niched into this super cool sector of lymphedema in true Projector style. She's fully booked out in her practice but added another income stream of selling compression garments. Mostly socks. She's making ground talking to her existing customers about compression garments as they visit her. Imagine an automated email sequence for all her customers that told them about her offer (other than the appointments.) Or figure out a way to reach strangers through social media.

Projectors will naturally build trust with their audience once they get their attention. So, when you have their attention, make sure you are using CTA's to your offers all the time. Don't be shy! People filter out what they aren't ready for, so don't worry, you will come off too salesy. Remember, if they're hanging out with you, you're already invited.

Pre-scheduling content can be tricky. Live is always going to perform better than scheduled. It comes down to energy. The most exciting energy is going to be closest to your aura. When you create content that goes into a scheduler, make sure you are doing it in response to an invitation. Part of the vibe of a Projector is that they know stuff. You already have a wise aura, so you can pre-schedule content that supports your influence, like some of your teaching content.

Another thing to consider: Don't re-invent the wheel with your content all the time. Observe what content gets the best engagement and re-schedule those posts. (If possible, port the comments and likes to add energetic momentum.) If you feel at all weird or icky making your offer, remind yourself you are a bad-ass mofo who all of us are waiting on to get your shit together and make an offer already. From this place of recognition of your bad-assery, create several posts that are just directing people to your offers. Get like 10 of them (the more, the better.) Put them in a scheduler on repeat so you don't have to think about it all the time. I like www.recurpost.com for this purpose because you can create decks of posts that rotate. When they get to the end, it starts at the beginning. So, make some, dump them in there. If a post flops, delete it.

Setting up your business to maximize your passions is critical. I want you to think for a moment about what your ideal working situation is. What type of offers appeals to you? What offers do you have now? Do you feel like they are successful? Is your business financially successful, and in what ways? What elements are not so successful? How many people do you want to work with each month? Are there patterns to when you have a surge of energy? What type of interaction with customers feel successful? Are there things that drain your energy?

When you plan out how your offers fit together and into your business, you want to consider that content will fulfil different roles. The idea of a customer journey should help your customers get to know you, trust you and be willing to pull out their wallets to purchase what you offer.

There are four things that content does in your business:

1. **Attract**: This is your freebies, social media presence, and ads.
   Now that you're using Human Design, you know that you are the
   niche that attracts your customers, so this content should represent
   your passions, quirks, and values. All this content needs to do is
   get them interested enough to learn more.
2. **Nurture:** This content is your email sequences, social media
   presence, small and mid-level offers, and other valuable content.
   This should grow your relationship with your customer. The email
   sequence is where you share stories, values, give away more good
   stuff, and prepare them to be warm when you have something to
   sell. This goes the same for social media. Small and mid-level
   offers (up to about $300) are relationship building when they buy
   that product and find out how amazing your stuff is, that it is
   perfect for them, and you are the person they want to learn from.
   If you do your mid-level offers well, you have customers for life.
3. **Convert:** You have to have content that asks for the sale. Which
   means you need to be clear about what you're selling. For me,
   getting clear about who I am, what I stand for, and how I want to
   fulfil my purpose in this world came from learning more about my
   energy dynamics, healing shadows, and following satisfaction.
   Then things clicked into place; I didn't have to force the message
   out. I just had to speak words true to my energy, and people are
   attracted to me in weird and wonderful ways. But sales are still
   not something that feel natural to me. I still have to make sure that
   my customer journey gives people calls to action at the
   appropriate times to lead them towards my more significant
   offers.
4. **Deliver:** Once you have sales, you need to deliver what you
   promised. Most of the time, this content feels the easiest to you.
   Just make sure that you use some of your energy to feed the
   machine and create content that does the other things too, OK?

I'd like to bust one myth that *all* you need is a high ticket offer. This seems to be the standard advice going around coaching circles. And while I agree that a high ticket offer is a good approach for coaches and course creators, it's tough to pull off if you don't have a few other offers that build trust and feed the funnel. Sales is a numbers game. The smaller offers don't make as much money, but their purpose is to have people who will give you the time of day about your high ticket offer. The fact is that to sell a high ticket offer, you need a relationship. And, you build relationship through building the journey with a customer. Someone may skip the lower stuff and go straight to your discovery call. But, they are rarely willing to do this without the foreplay, so to speak.

ADVERTIZING FOR PROJECTORS

ADS ARE ABOUT AMPLIFYING MOMENTUM. Before you go any further, you have to HAVE TO recognize yourself as an authority on your topic. If you don't feel confident that you are the person to solve your customers' problems, then ads are a waste of money for you. You've got this! You were born for this. Let that sink into your cells. Connect with that feeling every day before you do anything business-y.

Ads are tricky for Projectors. You and Generators have pretty much the same energy for ads. The typical ads that go directly to a sales page are initiating. That's Manifestor territory. You are magic once someone is part of your world, but the outside world needs to know you before they will respond to your ads. Ads are going to work great on your warm audience. Re-targeting ads are your best friend. But it does pose a problem when you want to use ads to grow your audience.

Ads are about amplifying momentum. Look at your organic posts and see what things attract the most engagement. Those are good indicators of the content that will appeal to your people. Once they are in your realm, anything goes with ads. Often Projectors have the most trouble getting people into their world in the first place. I'm going to invite you to consider three things regarding ads. Use your authority to consider how or if you use it in your business.

1. **Boosted Post.** Yeah, yeah, yeah, I know. I've heard the naysayers that a boosted post is just helping Zuck buy his thousandth beach home. But, consider this: you need to convey your message, your truth, and attract people, and you can't if they have never seen anything you create. Consider what you have been recognized for when you create content. That is likely the type you want to amplify with ads. If you find that some of that content is killing it in your community, that's the content that you should try to amplify. Find a post that had lots of engagement. I'm not talking engagement from your mom. I mean engagement from your actual target customers. When you boost it, make sure you copy the engagement (it's literally just a checkbox in ads manager.) You have your energy, the energy of people in your community who responded to that post, and now you're using that momentum to reach strangers. Make sure there is a small call to action (link to a freebie, or join you on social, etc.)

2. **Thought Reversal Ad**. This type of ad uses values to call out your ideal client. It helps them shift a belief, and because of this, it is a powerful way to attract customers.

This is how it works:

- Take an industry standard and talk about how it is the old way or the wrong way. You can pick a limiting belief, but an industry standard will help you stand out from others in your niche.

- Empathize, saying you understand why they think that way.
- Discredit the common thought or belief. Usually, this looks like pointing out the flaw in logic. Typically it goes something like this: if everyone followed that advice, we should all have full coaching schedules and full courses, and people doing other things would fail. (Be more subtle than this, please. It was for effect. Soften it with your details.)
- Illustrate the story of what happens when you stay with that type of thinking
- Call to Action to the new way

- **Story Ad** or ad that shows your **credibility.** These are probably two different types of ads, but it is awesome if you can use them both together. Think of a story that your ideal customer can empathize and relate to. (This is what they are going through right now that you can help them with.) Layer on the authority by telling them details like your experience solving this problem or share results from your customers. Make sure you have a CTA. It isn't that different from a boosted post. In fact, most of your social media posts will follow some form of storytelling, and when you add a CTA, that makes it an ad.

One place to look for inspiration (and to heal shadows) is the gate and line of your Unconscious Moon. In Gene Keys, it is the Attraction Sphere. It can give you insight into the qualities, values, and type of content that will attract your people and help build a relationship. It can also show you where you might need to do some healing work so that you can actually attract people from a clear frequency. Also, conscious sun gate because it's your strongest energy.

Momentum is the most crucial thing in attracting customers. You have your own energy and momentum, but your community and content will also create and add to it. In my opinion, this explains why the big names can do pretty much anything where advertising is concerned. They have created sufficient momentum, and their community gives them authority, adding different pieces of energy to the content, making it more appealing to a broader audience.

Building an audience becomes much easier the more people you have in your community. Once people are in your community, you can sell to them. You attract people by holding your frequency by speaking your truth loud and proud, and customers come to you. That's the secret. But, if you look for ways to amplify your momentum, that's how you get quantum results. It's about combining energy AND strategy.

MONEY IN YOUR BUSINESS

NO MATTER YOUR ENERGY TYPE, you will want to have some safety structures built-in. In her book Big Magic (which should be required reading for anyone wanting to earn money off their creativity), Elizabeth Gilbert says that you need to treat your (creative project of whatever type) like a baby. Let it grow and learn and figure itself out before you expect it to pay the bills.

I know this is counter to what you hear all over the internet: people go from nothing to 6 figures in a month. While that can happen, it's not typical, and if you're expecting your income from a new business to support you right out of the gate, it's going to put a lot of pressure on you and your creation. Do you work well under pressure? Do you love what you're doing when you're under pressure? Maybe you do, but for me, that's not the case. Diversifying your income streams is one of the best ways to create stability so that you can get your business off the ground and get through the low ebbs in energy without being stressed out or feeling like you have to do something to bring money in. Just a little disclaimer, I'm not a financial advisor and don't claim to be. Make aligned

decisions about your money, and get the right professional advice. The discussion below is food for thought.

1. **Semi-passive income:** Your money is where your energy is, so "passive income" is a bit of a misnomer. You will always have to feed energy into passive income projects at times. This might look like hiring someone to help maintain your passive products or directing your attention towards them on occasion to boost their energy. You could also consider re-packaging content you have already created as bonuses in your current ventures. When you re-purpose content, make sure the product aligns with your message. Something else to consider is packaging some of your older stuff (or creating something especially for the purpose) into upsells, downsells, order bumps, etc. If you are trying to create passive income, remember that it will take maintenance, whether from your energy or someone else's.

2. **Affiliate Marketing:** This can take a lot of work, but the way I recommend it is that you have a few products that you recommend to your audience with affiliate links. Make them part of your existing customer journey, and you can capture some profit by piggybacking on your current marketing structures. You could also consider affiliate marketing on a larger scale. For example, you sell the course, and someone else fulfils it. I'm sure you've seen this with the big names. If you're good at attracting people to your message but don't feel like it's the right thing to offer a signature program, this could be a good option for you.

3. **Investments**: Find an advisor you jive with, and let their energy manage it. One of the best financial lessons is the power of compound interest. Set a regular withdrawal, and forget about it, even if it's a small amount. Don't watch and worry about it all the time. You access it later, and it will need time to grow. Unlike property, this type of investment is usually liquid unless the fund is locked for some reason, usually tax reasons. Your advisor

should help you figure out your risk tolerance and choose an investment right for you.

4. **Income property:** Property has its own energy. So do renters. If this is an option for you, think about the logistics of the property you purchase. Are you OK with the occasional sounds, smells, and sharing of outdoor space of renting out a basement apartment? Suppose you don't live at the property. Are you willing to hire someone to manage it or be available yourself for the emergencies and maintenance that come up, usually at inconvenient times? You can rent rooms or suites via Airbnb or similar sites to earn cash and not have the long-term renter situation, but then the turnover presents another thing to manage. Another way property can make you money is by living in a place long enough to give you equity. You only access equity when you sell your home but typically re-invest it in another place to live. Equity isn't really the type of money you can rely on to provide stability unless you're willing to sell your property.

Managing your money is an integral part of business. Reducing the emotional reactivity around it is typically the first and most important step. The majority of what I do is help people manage the emotional roller coaster of business in my small group and 1:1 containers. Find out more here: **http://carmenfarrellknapp.com/workwithme**. You also want to think of ways to use your money to serve and support you rather than being at its mercy.

Signing off and a few CTA's

I have other books in this series that are the bomb once you use your strategy and authority consistantly. The logical next step is the book in this series "Finding your Business Mojo with Human Design." This is where I really dive into leveraging your unique energy in your messaging and marketing. For example, where to look in your chart on who you might be best positioned to serve, how you best communicate, and how to use it to create your messaging.

Obvi, you can find me on social media. Handles change, but my name won't, so you can search me out as Carmen Farrell Knapp. I would love to hang out with you in the online world. Let me know how you're using Human Design in your business.

BOOK FOUR

GENERATORS AND MANIFESTING GENERATORS

DEFINED SACRAL CENTERS.
MG'S HAVE A MOTOR CENTER CONNECTED TO THE THROAT
AND DEFINED SACRAL

Generators and Manifesting Generators

To Respond	Frustration	Satisfaction
	MG's Frustration + Anger = Impatience	
STRATEGY	NOT SELF THEME	SELF THEME

You are here to build, create, and work. Your secret sauce is going to come from doing what you love. When you find your message and purpose, you are unstoppable! Your sacral motor gives you consistent energy to create. Generators are amazing at mastering a process over time. You are methodical and learn how to master each step of a process and teach others to do the same. Manifesting Generators are here to find the efficiencies. You are an express builder who skips steps and creates things fast.

You have a natural resilience because skipping steps involves finding steps that you can't cut. You have a built-in trial and error to your process. You can find shortcuts and teach others how to get there fast.

If you're an MG reading this, all the Generator information applies to you. When appropriate, I separate and highlight the stuff that's different. This book is about using your energy, and the foundational practice of Human Design, which for you is identical to a Generator. So, from here on, assume I mean you when I say Generator.

INTRODUCTION TO BEING A
GENERATOR OR MG

MG'S and Generators operate exactly the same in Strategy and Authority. Some schools of thought suggest MG's are a hybrid between the Manifestor and the Generator and should add a step of informing to their process. While MG's have the similarity of having a motor connected by a channel to the throat, they should not operate as Manifestors, even though that energetic channel will give you the urge to inform and initiate. Don't do it. It is only going to lead to further course correction down the road. In my opinion, (and in my experience as an MG), it makes no sense to add a step when you cut steps out.

It is also very easy to go from informing to initiating, which will take the MG out of their power of responding and lead to many frustrating situations. While your not-self theme is always frustration, watch when you are impatient or trying to push or force something to happen. It's a sign that you are in Manifestor territory.

. . .

A word about conditioning for Generators: unless you have very aware and in tune parents, you were probably raised to initiate like a Manifestor. Generators have a lot of energy. Usually, this means that you were told to just go and do things as a child. Make it happen. Use your energy to do it, regardless of resistance. Generators respond to their environment and tune in to their internal guidance system (which will be either bringing awareness to their emotional wave or listening to the intuitive hit of their sacral.) Many people Don't know how to listen to inner awareness, or even worse, *gasp* your emotions. It takes time to build your trust and confidence in following your inner authority, and sometimes it is subtle unless you attune to its communication.

Defined Sacral will give you a lot of energy, and it will be consistently available. It is considered life force energy and means you are hardwired to respond to things that give you an outlet to create, build and do. There is a myth that you are an energizer bunny with a sacral motor. This is not a good descriptor. When you are doing something you love, you can get immersed in it and have a lot of available energy, but it's not inexhaustible. And, when you're doing things that misalign to Strategy and Authority, it will drain that energy quickly. A Generator should fully use their energy supply during the day. If you consider what sacral energy is available for (creativity, vitality, sexuality), it becomes very important to follow your responses to things that help you feel alive, and quite literally, turn you on.

If you experience insomnia or poor sleep quality, it is an indication that you aren't using your energy up entirely, or you are using it on things that are draining to you. It is important to wait until you are tired before going to bed for Generators. Unlike non-energy types, it's not a good idea to "wind down" in bed for you.

. . .

Generators experience regular plateaus in their life and business. If the plateau goes on for an extended time, it becomes a void. In human design terms, we say that a Generator reaches mastery and then takes a break. Some people will experience it regularly and can plan for it. And… sometimes it comes at the most inconvenient times. You might even go so far as to call it burnout. In any other energy type, we would.

Your sacral energy is, at least in part, physical energy, and even in a plateau, doesn't completely shut off. So, you have this trickle of energy that often allows you to push through. If you also have an activated spleen, your body and immune system tend to be strong. It can take a lot to take you down. Once the mighty tree has fallen, you recover pretty quickly, at least to functional levels. Functional does not mean optimal. I'm just going to say it: Generators take the strength in their physical body for granted.

When you run out of energy, "taking a break" or at least slowing down for a time isn't optional. There are healthy ways to do your plateau times like resting, recuperating, mentally giving yourself a break, and changing pace. Then there's those of us (me, for example) who try to push through it. One practice that is important in general for Generators, especially when they're in the plateau, is to ground yourself in the physical body. Take time to feel, breathe, listen. Know that your head will guilt trip you into moving sooner than you should, so keep bringing your attention back to the present moment and your physical experience. Follow your strategy and authority, which will get you through your plateaus. Do something that makes you feel satisfied. Perhaps you can even learn to enjoy your plateaus instead of pushing through them as quickly as you can.

Strategy: To Respond

Life will bring you everything that is meant for you if you wait for it. I know. I hate waiting too. But, you know what's worse? Making decisions that ultimately lead to frustration. There is never a shortage of things to respond to, but often we aren't attuned to the present moment enough to notice them. I used to think that " Generator" was a reference between the sacral motor and a power generator. It actually refers to the generated field that makes up a Generator's aura. This generated field is what magnetizes things to respond to. The generated field will be a particular frequency that attracts things, people, and situations. So, this is why Generators need to maintain a clean energy field. What you're subconsciously constructing your aura of is what you will get more of to respond to.

You will want to be aware of a few things when you first start working with your strategy of response. Working with your strategy is more about being receptive and aware, and less about seeking and trying to logic your way to a specific outcome. The sacral center will give you a yes or no answer in response to your environment. Its purpose is to let you know whether your sacral energy is available for that thing or not. Even those with an Emotional Authority will have the sacral response.

Response is not the same as reaction. It's essential to be on to yourself about your triggers. Emotional regulation is how you keep yourself in response. This will mean elongating the space between the stimulus and action. It's true for both emotional and sacral authorities. Where in your business do you just react to situations? What about money? Are you triggered by money, lack of money, spending money, what others do with their money, how others make their money? What about in your relationships? Does social media trigger you?

·   ·   ·

The chances are that where you are reactive is somewhere you have some shadow work to take care of. Reacting comes from not-self behavior, and you want to bring your awareness to it, so you can choose to respond rather than react. It may take a bit of practice as well. The brain develops stronger neural pathways the more frequently a mental pattern is used. You may have practiced your responses to triggers since childhood, so be kind to yourself, but keep calling yourself out for reactivity.

Let me back up for a minute. Most of what you hear in the business world is hyper masculine, goal-oriented, mind and ego-driven. Make a goal, go out, and make it happen. Yeah. That's not going to work for you. Why? Because your energy doesn't initiate. Now, before you say that Manifestors have it easy in business, hold up a minute.

Your energy has amazing business potential if you know how to use it right. Instead of going out into the world to seek out the things (clients, programs, message) you need, you will (naturally, without effort) draw the resources, tools, people, and experiences you need to you through your aura. You will generate an aura that brings you everything you need if you live your truth and do the things you love. Love your quirkiness, follow your passion, and the world opens up.

Manifestors don't have a warm, friendly aura that people are drawn. Your aura is very open and welcoming. In fact, when you align your business to your purpose, passion, and gifts, you will never be short of customers to serve. The basic priority is to get yourself aligned with using your energy. This will put you on the same frequency as what you want. You don't go out and get it. You let it come to you. But, you need to align yourself to the frequency that "it" is. You do this by responding to what your strategy brings you to respond to and authority guides you towards.

· · ·

For those with sacral authority, you will get a response and act in the moment. Emotional authorities will take the sacral response and put it through your emotional wave to ensure it is still a yes even when you're at a high, neutral, and low emotional state. Either way, watch for the emotion of excitement as an indicator that you are on the right path.

You can develop your awareness of the sacral response by asking yourself or having someone ask you yes or no questions and answer from the body. Do this with inconsequential things to practice. While having a friend or coach ask you the Y/N questions is a good way of figuring out your response, and getting a handle on a situation, try to learn not to rely on it. The sacrum will often give you physical clues like leaning towards or away from or making uh-huh/uh -un noises. Ideally, you develop the muscle of knowing what your sacral is communicating, so you are self-sufficient in your decision-making without needing to be asked questions all the time. It also means that you respond to your environment rather than a contrived set up of questions. This means that you learn how to observe the things that life is presenting to you.

Finally, not all sacral yeses are made equal. Just because you have the energy to respond to something doesn't mean you have to. Saying yes to something means you are committing your energy to it. Sometimes it is worth waiting for something that really lights you up before taking action. Your zone of genius is going to be doing what you LOVE doing. There is a difference between not minding doing something or kind of liking it to LOVING it, so sometimes, it is worth the wait to use your sacral energy on the big things. Just sayin'

AUTHORITY FOR GENERATORS
AND MG'S

AUTHORITY IS DETERMINED BY THE CENTER(S) YOU HAVE
DEFINED

AUTHORITY FOR GENERATORS AND MG'S

EMOTIONAL AUTHORITY (51% of the population)

This is the most common authority. About 50% of the population has an emotional authority. While it is common, most people are unaware of how to use the information and fuel that a defined solar plexus can give you. It is an awareness center for emotional processing and one of the 4 "motors" in the body graph. Using this authority takes time to process emotions, and you guessed it, awareness of the highs and lows of the wave.

Emotional authority is NOT figuring out how you feel about a decision and making decisions based on emotion.

It is about using the different emotions of your emotional wave as information to come to clarity. You feel your way through the highs and lows of emotions about that decision until you just know what the right path is.

The emotional wave is a mechanical process. You will have a stimulus that you respond to that triggers an emotion that you follow through the high, low, and between. This isn't avoidable. You will have an emotional wave regardless. You can suppress or enhance emotion, but it happens whether you want to experience it or not. The best-case scenario is that you learn to use emotion as the experience and tool it is for you and then allow it to flow through you. They can get stuck when you try to repress emotions, creating an elongated wave. Part of your routine should be to feel the emotions of that moment and see if you can feel where you are resisting emotion. Allow yourself to feel in a safe space if there are emotionally unresolved feelings.

The thing with emotion is that your mind and ego will want to get involved and label it as good or bad, this or that, and you will start to create stories around the emotional experience. Ego wants to move you out of discomfort as quickly as possible, but much of your growth as an entrepreneur will come from your superpower of being able to ride out the wave of discomfort. If you can learn not to identify with your emotions and mine the truth they have to tell you, then you will be unstoppable! Much of this work is awareness about what you make your emotions mean and allowing them to flow without creating resistance.

The key with the emotional wave is to make sure you have come to neutral before deciding. Does this mean you need to ride out the emotional wave on every decision? NO! But be aware of when you feel triggered (high or low) and wait until you have more emotional clarity. Most people can understand not deciding from a low part of the wave, but it's equally important to avoid the high state. Think of a time when you've been super excited about something. You commit on the spot and find that after, when you aren't on the top of the wave, you don't actually have the energy, or it is something that you aren't that passionate about, but... you said yes and are stuck seeing it through.

Depending on which channel(s) are defined for you will give your wave a different flavor. If you have multiple channels defined, you can experience the wave differently. The type of wave will also determine what you are available to direct your energy towards. Decisions of this nature will be important to give yourself the time to process and ride out the wave, as these are the types of decisions that will have the most power for you. Not everything that inspires you is super important, but the things that are hardwired for you to be initiated by are determined by the active channels in your authority. When you look at which channels are creating your emotional wave, you can also look up information on the circuitry it belongs to and the channel and gates to better understand what will initiate your process.

While your strategy is to respond, your authority will tell you if you have the energy available for it. Unlike a sacral authority which is a clear yes or no, you will rarely be 100% sure because you have to feel out the decision through the high and low and everything in between your emotional wave. So for you, pretty sure is good enough. Be aware of when your mind starts to try to sway you one way or another. Stick with the feeling you get from a decision, not the thoughts, stories, and drama.

The solar plexus is an awareness center for emotional energy. You will experience emotional energy in a specific, defined way. It will be unique to you but reliable, consistent, and predictable. You will seek things that give you an emotional experience because this is part of how you experience the world, learn, and grow. If you have this center defined, you are here to live a robust, vibrant, and varied emotional life.

Your inner authority will respond to the experiences, relationships, and things that let you play out the emotional experience. But, your emotional wave won't respond to *every* stimulus. The type of circuitry will give you a clue as to what you are hardwired to respond to in life (see the types of waves for more on that specifically.) But, your authority will give you a yes or a no, not a why. Your mind and ego will not be satisfied. So, there is a practice of quieting the mind in following your authority.

Your emotions enhance your life, and you can utilize the energy of emotion to create. Most of us have been socialized to view emotion as something to be restrained, resisted, or, worst case, be ashamed of. So it can be a completely new concept to some to allow emotion to have the deciding vote in how you do life. The first step is to start to become aware of your emotions. Notice if a specific emotion signals the start of your wave. Observe how you move through your wave with different triggers. Start to develop your vocabulary on your emotions, and notice the nuances between similar emotions. Journaling can help with this. Another technique is to check in with yourself at each meal, morning and night, and notice what you feel. The more awareness you bring to your emotions, the better you will understand how to work with this powerful, amazing energy.

Here are a few things to keep in mind when working with emotional energy:

- An emotion is just a vibration in the body. Some of the more intense emotional energy like anxiety, or even excitement, will pass through you. The chemical spike an emotion creates in your blood lasts approximately 90 seconds. So, if you can stay with the feeling, observing yourself and breathing through it, it will flow through you. If you resist or fight emotion, that spike can extend, or worse, rebound with more intensity.
- Most of working with emotional energy is learning not to resist.

Allow it to flow, observe how you feel through the whole experience, come to neutral, then act. Resistance can cause your emotional energy to get stuck, and this is how you can potentially experience extended times in lower vibration emotions like depression.

- Avoid labeling emotions as positive or negative. The energy of emotion is neutral until you assign meaning to it with thoughts. You are designed to experience the whole range of emotions, not just the "positive" ones. Taking the mindset of observing the sensation of emotions in your body will help.

When you are around people without definition in the solar plexus, they will pick up on your emotional wave (whether they know it or not!) and amplify it back to you. While you can share your emotions with others, your emotional wave is yours, and if you are trying to work through something, it is best to do it out of the energy of others.

Types of Emotional Wave

The Source of all Waves: Solar Plexus to Sacral: 6-59: Channel of Intimacy

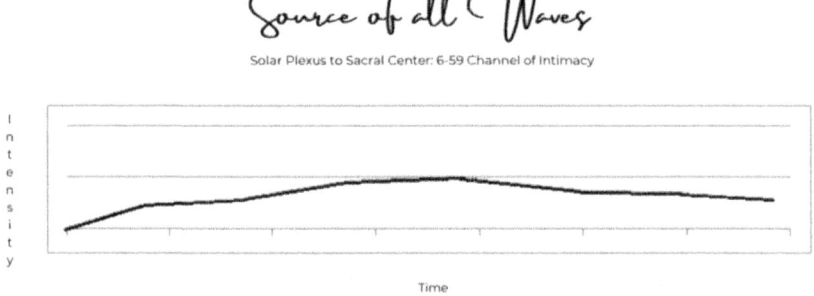

Source of all Waves

Solar Plexus to Sacral Center: 6-59 Channel of Intimacy

The source of all waves is about the intimacy in relationships that

allows people to create something new. It will respond to relationships that can lead to the creativity to build or create. The channel is called the channel of mating, or intimacy, and can refer to creating new life or any other creative process between 2 people. This wave responds to the things that create a connection between people. It will flow up then plateau with each connection. It is a gentle rise, plateau, then drift back down. The theme is about human connection, responding to relationships, and seeking out the connections that will lead to something new. It is a reasonably gentle wave and very good at relating to others. Anyone with this channel will be a Generator and will want to follow the relationships that lead them to create things they are passionate about.

Tribal Wave: Solar Plexus to Root: 49-19: Channel of Synthesis and Solar Plexus to Heart: 37-40: Channel of Community

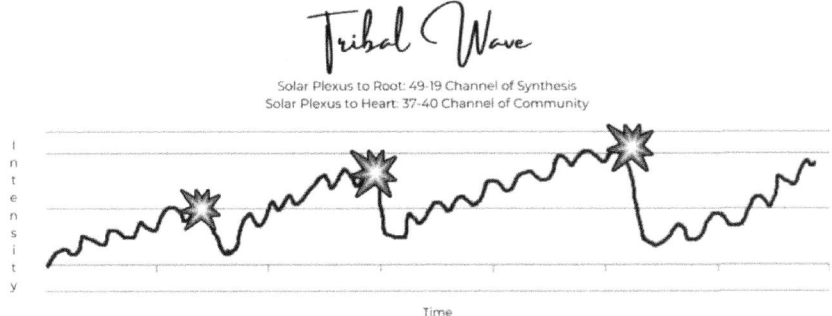

The tribal wave will respond to survival or need in the intimate community. It is part of the tribal circuitry. It responds to the needs of the tribe or family (tribal is different from collective, which is concerned with the greater good, tribal is concerned with the survival and thriving of people in the close circle.) It is concerned with resources and providing the tools you and your tribe need to survive.

Physical connection is a key component to this wave, and when you are triggered, it will help you ground yourself to connect physically. It operates like a ratchet. You are triggered, then relax back, kind of like you shake it off. It may take a few times before you reach the explosion point, but you will eventually get agitated enough by the trigger to have a release of emotion. Then there will be a reset. This wave is not subtle and can feel a bit out of control at times. Being aware of how this wave operates and your typical responses will help you find positive ways to release the emotional energy. Do you pick a fight so that you can hug it out? Perhaps it would be easier to ask for a hug. Just sayin'

The Individual Wave: Solar Plexus to Root: 55-39:Channel of Emoting, Solar Plexus to Throat 22-12: Channel of Openness

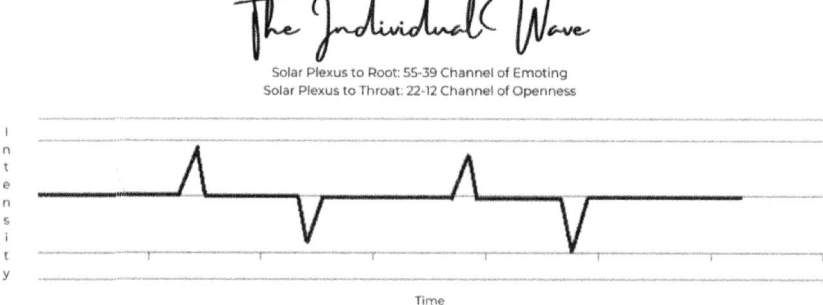

The individual wave is characterized by passion. Your mood is how you express this wave. It can be a moody wave, and at times you will want to share this emotion with others, and at times it is best kept just for your experience alone. It has peaks then comes back to steadiness, then it drops, then comes back to steady. You want to be conscious of when you need time alone to feel your emotions without the influence of others. This will help you avoid getting trapped in the lows and keep moving with the mood. It is important to allow yourself space, connect to your needs and desires, and learn how to ground yourself when it gets a little too wavy. The channels of this wave are part of the individual circuitry and will respond to the things that help you grow and advance as an individual.

The Abstract Wave: Solar Plexus to Root: 30-41: Channel of Recognition, Solar Plexus to Throat: 36-35: Chanel of Transitoriness

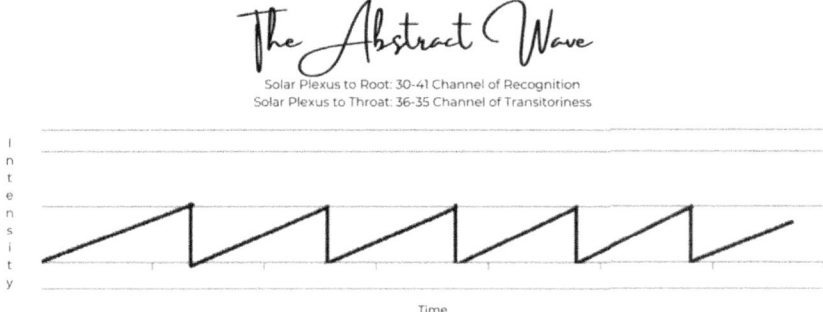

Solar Plexus to Root: 30-41 Channel of Recognition
Solar Plexus to Throat: 36-35 Channel of Transitoriness

There will be a gentler rhythm to this wave than the individual wave. It will ebb and flow by responding to experience. The two channels associated with this wave carry a great deal of friction. The 35-36 seeks new beginnings and wants to respond to the things worth pursuing, and the 30-41 communicates the lessons learned through overcoming friction through emotion. Remember that this is your natural energetic state, so following strategy and authority and allowing this wave to operate as it is meant will help you determine the worthwhile conflict and holds the vision and optimism that each experience brings. This wave can present challenges when you enter into an experience with an expectation that is not met, causing an emotional crash. It is important not to attach yourself to an outcome Rather, you are going into an experience for the sake of the emotion it will create and the things you can learn from it.

Sacral Authority (32.6% of the population)

Only Generators will have a sacral authority. If you have this authority, you will be able to make decisions in the moment. This means you can get feedback from the sacrum and act right away. There will be a physical response from the sacrum to indicate a yes or no. If you get feedback that is a "maybe" or "kind of," consider it a no for now until you get a clear response. There is nothing subtle about your yes. You will feel excited or drawn to act in a certain way, and it will feel natural for you to do so.

If you're not used to following your sacral response, building trust in your response can take some time. It will tell you yes or no, but it won't explain itself. It won't be like you should walk your dog in the park today instead of the usual route because that's where you will meet your future partner. It will present as a leaf blowing across your path in front of the entrance to the park. The sacral will say walk in the park. The stimulus that you respond to can be inconsequential, or something big like an article about moving to Italy, a friend's illness that prompts you to apply to med school, or something you read that makes you change your mind about your marketing plan.

Sometimes, the seemingly inconsequential things can lead you to respond to big, life-changing, and amazing things. Don't worry about what you're responding to so much as what your sacral says to do in response.

The sacral will give you a physical response. You feel sacral energy in your body. Many people spent most of their life trying to control and ignore the physical body. It is an ongoing learning process to stay grounded in the physical body to hear the sacrum's subtle communication. Even if you have an emotional authority, your defined sacral will give you physical feedback. You might notice yourself leaning towards or backing away from things. Sometimes it is described as a sensation in the low belly or a "gut" response. Much has been written about "sacral noises" of "uh-huh" and "uh-un" being indicators from the sacrum. There is also this weird middle ground noise of uhhhhhhh. This means either yes, but not now or undecided, so you need some more things for the sacral to respond to before it can give you a clear yes or no.

If your sacral has a direct channel to the spleen (34-57 or 27-50) your sacral response will be more instinctual. Your yes and no may be accompanied by a particular physical sensation like a tingling in your neck or your own version of spidy-sense. It may also influence what your sacral energy is available to respond to. This means you may have a natural survival drive and response powered by sacral energy. What it looks like is that you combine intuition with response. If you notice that you are experiencing a lot of fear about your response, it is an indication that the spleen is leading, so get back into the energy of the sacrum: Is my energy available for this or not. Then act… or don't.

Signature: Satisfaction Not-self theme: Frustration

Your signature is how you know you are on the right path. When you feel satisfied, you are following your strategy and making decisions from your authority. This is a good health check for your energy. If you are experiencing more Frustration than Satisfaction, you want to look at how you are making decisions and where you might be operating from conditioning and/or not-self.

As a Generator, you want to follow the things that leave you feeling satisfied. Your goals should center around things that lead to greater satisfaction. In my experience, your purpose and how you fulfill it is pretty damn satisfying. If you're curious about your purpose, check out the gates of your Incarnation Cross found in your conscious and unconscious sun and earth.

Your energy has specific things that it will respond to, and as a Generator, that is creating and building things and... sex. Sometimes an orgasm will do more for you than a nap; just sayin' Projectors have this weird thing with naps, can Generators claim the orgasm as our nap? Now that I've gone and made it weird let's get back to business.

GENERATOR GOALS

SATISFACTION IS the goal of a Generator. Doing what you love and loving what you do should be the tagline. Generators get satisfaction out of doing work. Take a look at your business. What are you satisfied with? What activities make you feel satisfied? What things lead to more frustration? When was the last time you felt satisfied with your marketing? Messaging? Offers? Community? Are you satisfied with your business model? Do you like what you're doing? What parts of your work do you not like doing? These are important questions for a Generator to reflect on. They will give you some direction when you set goals.

Goals can be challenging for Generators, particularly sacral authority because your energy works in the moment. All Generators respond to what life brings them. So, the typical advice about goal setting doesn't account for the unexpected things that come your way. But, goals are an essential part of running a business. It's how we measure how well things are working and figure out the elements that need adjustment.

You also want to set a focus for each 90-day segment in your business (you might align to the quarters, but if you're going all rebel on me, set your 90 days whenever you want.) Decide what element of your business you want to grow in this time. Is it audience growth? Is it messaging alignment? Is it reach? Is it traffic to your sales page or webinar? Set a target on your 90-day goal, but realize that there will be some flexibility in that metric as you progress towards it and have more things to respond to. When you have more information, update your goals.

You need to leave enough flexibility in your goals so that you can respond to the incredible things that come up. The problem with committing strongly to your goals in advance is that you lose your power to respond in the moment. Your authority will tell you if you have the energy to respond to something. Rigid goals will commit your energy in advance, leaving you tied up and unable to respond in the moment, or you find that you don't actually have energy for the things that you committed to.

Which means set the goals. But they need to be tended to along the way. FYI, I'm speaking as a Generator with a completely open will center, so you may have energy elsewhere in your chart that lets you do goals a little differently. In general, when you're setting goals, keep in mind that your power is in the moment, AND you need to have some direction in your business.

I guess that you've been burned by the typical (heavy-handed?) advice on goals in the past and are a bit hesitant to even set them. You can only set so many goals and not reach them before you start telling yourself a story about your abilities to achieve and goal set. Be real, have you given up on goals? My advice to you is to shift your mindset about goals. You want to have high-level navigational goals. The SMART goal people will probably hunt me down for this, but leave them vague. They can be dreamy and fuzzy. One of my high-level goals is to have a business with a 2x/year launch for a signature program or mastermind and a few 1:1 clients. Traditional goal advice would want me to start filling in the details, give it a deadline and assign measurements of success. It's OK if you don't.

BUSINESS MODELS FOR GENERATORS

THE THINGS that draw the most money in for you are the things you are focused on and passionate about in the moment. Money follows energy. I hope this didn't burst any bubbles about the dream of passive income. You will probably find that live launches are more effective than evergreen. If you're a course creator, the programs you are actively involved in or marketing are likely your biggest yielding. Basically, you need to be present to use your superpowers of response. When there is direct access to your energy, clients will follow.

The same principle applies to pre-scheduling your content. The best-case scenario is that you post on your social channels in response to things in your environment. I realize this isn't practical all of the time, but the content you pre-schedule, make sure that you are creating it in response, but just publishing it later. Also, engage with people commenting on your posts. That way, you can inject fresh energy into that post. If you choose to outsource this part, at least occasionally comment on your and other people's posts. Your ideal customers want to sample what it's like to be part of your world, and your motto for social media should be "welcome to the party!"

Your profile is like the suit you wear in your business. Lean into your profile when thinking of how to create content. For example, a 3 line will do well with sharing experiences, while a 1 might do better with a "what to do post."

Setting up your business to maximize your passions is critical. You will want to find ways to do the things you love the most and outsource the things that tire or frustrate you. I want you to think for a moment about what your ideal working situation is. What type of offers appeal to you? What offers do you have now? Are they satisfying? Do they bring in a satisfying amount of money? What even is a satisfying amount of money? What elements are not so satisfying? How many people do you want to work with each month?

When you plan out how your offers fit together and into your business, you want to consider that content will fulfill different roles in your business. The idea of a customer journey should help your customers get to know you, trust you and be willing to pull out their wallets to purchase what you offer.

There are four things that content does in your business:

1.   **Attract**: This is your freebies, social media presence, and ads. Now that you're using Human Design, you know that you are the niche that attracts your customers, so this content should represent your passions, quirks, and values. All this content needs to do is get them interested enough to learn more.

2. **Nurture:** This content is your email sequences, social media presence, small and mid-level offers, and other valuable content. This should grow your relationship with your customer. The email sequence is where you share stories, values, give away more good stuff, and prepare them to be warm when you have something to sell. This goes the same for social media. Small and mid-level offers (up to about $300) are relationship building when they buy that product and find out how amazing your stuff is, that it is perfect for them, and you are the person they want to learn from. If you do your mid-level offers well, you have customers for life.

3. **Convert:** You have to have content that asks for the sale. Which means you need to be clear about what you're selling. For me, getting clear about who I am, what I stand for, and how I want to fulfill my purpose in this world came from learning more about my energy dynamics, healing shadows, and following satisfaction. Then things clicked into place; I didn't have to force the message out. I just had to speak words true to my energy, and people are attracted to me in weird and wonderful ways. But sales are still not something that feel natural to me. I still have to make sure that my customer journey gives people calls to action at the appropriate times to lead them towards my more significant offers.

4. **Deliver:** Once you have sales, you need to deliver what you promised. Most of the time, this content feels the easiest to you. Just make sure that you use some of your energy to feed the machine and create content that does the other things too, OK?

I'd like to bust one myth that *all* you need is a high ticket offer. This seems to be the standard advice going around coaching circles. And while I agree that a high ticket offer is a good idea, it's tough to pull off if you don't have a few other offers that build trust and feed the funnel. Sales is a numbers game. The smaller offers don't make as much money, but their purpose is to have people who will give you the time of day about your high ticket offer. The fact is that to sell a high ticket offer, you need a relationship. And, you build relationship through building the journey with a customer. Someone may skip the lower stuff and go straight to your discovery call. But, they are rarely willing to do this without the foreplay, so to speak.

ADVERTIZING FOR GENERATORS

ADS ARE TRICKY FOR GENERATORS. The typical ads that go directly to a sales page are initiating. That's Manifestor territory. You are magic once someone is part of your world, but the outside world needs to know you before they will respond to your ads. Ads are going to work great on your warm audience. Re-targeting ads are your best friend. But it does pose a problem when you want to use ads to grow your audience.

Ads are about amplifying momentum. Look at your organic posts and see what things attract the most engagement. Those are good indicators of the content that will appeal to your people. Once they are in your realm, anything goes with ads. Often Generators have the most trouble getting people into their world in the first place. I'm going to give you three things to respond to. Use your authority to consider how or if you use it in your business.

1.   **Boosted Post.** Yeah, yeah, yeah, I know. I've heard the naysayers that a boosted post is just helping Zuck buy his thousandth beach home. But,

consider this: you need to convey your message, your truth, and attract people, and you can't if they have never seen anything you create. Content should always be in response, but if you find that some of that content is killing it in your community, that's the content that you should try to amplify. Find a post that had lots of engagement. I'm not talking engagement from your mom. I mean engagement from your actual target customers. When you boost it, make sure you copy the engagement (it's literally just a checkbox in ads manager.) You have your energy, the energy of people in your community who responded to that post, and now you're using that momentum to reach strangers. Make sure there is a small call to action (link to a freebie or join you on social etc.)

2.   **Thought Reversal Ad**. This type of ad uses values to call out your ideal client. It helps them shift a belief, and because of this, it is a powerful way to attract customers.

This is how it works:

- Take an industry standard and talk about how it is the old way or the wrong way. You can pick a limiting belief, but an industry standard will help you stand out from others in your niche.
- Empathize, saying you understand why they think that way.
- Discredit the common thought or belief. Usually, this looks like pointing out the flaw in logic. Typically it goes something like this: if everyone followed that advice, we should all have full coaching schedules and full courses, and people doing other things would fail. (Be more subtle than this, please. It was for effect. Soften it with your details.)
- Illustrate the story of what happens when you stay with that type of thinking
- Call to Action to the new way

3.   **Story Ad** or ad that shows your **credibility**. These are probably two separate types of ads, but it is awesome if you can use them both together. Think of a story that your ideal customer can empathize and relate to. (This is what they are going through right now that you can help them with.) Layer on the authority by telling them details like your experience solving this problem or share the results of your clients. Make sure you have a CTA. It isn't that different from a boosted post. Most of your social media posts will follow some form of storytelling, and when you add a CTA, that makes it an ad.

One place to look for inspiration (and to heal shadows) is the gate and line of your Unconscious Moon. In Gene Keys, it is the Attraction Sphere. It can give you some insight into the qualities, values, and type of content that will attract your people and help build relationships. It can also show you where you might need to do some healing work so that you can actually attract people from a clear frequency.

Momentum is the most crucial thing in attracting customers. You have your energy and momentum, but your community and content will also create and add to it. In my opinion, this explains why the big names can do pretty much anything where advertising is concerned. They have created sufficient momentum, and their community gives them authority, adding different pieces of energy to the content, making it more appealing to a broader audience.

Building an audience becomes much easier, the more people you have in your community. Once people are in your community, you can sell to them. You attract people by holding your frequency by speaking your truth loud and proud, and customers come to you. That's the secret. But, if you look for ways to amplify your momentum, that's how you get quantum results. It's about combining energy AND strategy.

CARMEN FARRELL-KNAPP

MONEY IN YOUR BUSINESS

REGARDLESS OF YOUR ENERGY TYPE, you will want to have some built-in safety structures. In her book Big Magic (which should be required reading for anyone wanting to earn money off their creativity), Elizabeth Gilbert says that you need to treat your (creative project of whatever type) like a baby. Let it grow and learn and figure itself out before you expect it to pay the bills.

I know this is counter to what you hear all over the internet: people go from nothing to 6 figures in a month. While that can happen, it's not typical, and if you're expecting your income from a new business to support you right out of the gate, it's going to put a lot of pressure on you and your creation. Do you work well under pressure? Do you love what you're doing when you're under pressure? Maybe you do, but for me, that's not the case. Diversifying your income streams is one of the best ways to create stability so that you can get your business off the ground and get through the low ebbs in energy without being stressed out or feeling like you have to do something to bring money in. Just a little disclaimer, I'm not a financial advisor and don't claim to be. Make aligned

decisions about your money, and get the right professional advice. The discussion below is food for thought.

1.   **Semi-passive income:** Your money is where your energy is, so "passive income" is a bit of a misnomer. You will always have to feed energy into passive income projects at times. This might look like hiring someone to help maintain your passive products or directing your attention towards them on occasion to boost their energy. You could also consider re-packaging content you have already created as bonuses in your current ventures. When you re-purpose content, make sure the product aligns with your message. Something else to consider is packaging some of your older stuff (or creating something especially for the purpose) into upsells, downsells, offer bumps, etc. If you are trying to create passive income, remember that it will take maintenance, whether from your energy or someone else's.

2.   **Affiliate Marketing:** This can take a lot of work, but the way I recommend it is that you have a few products that you recommend to your audience with affiliate links. Make them part of your existing customer journey, and you can capture some profit by piggybacking on your current marketing structures. You could also consider affiliate marketing on a larger scale. For example, you sell the course, and someone else fulfills it. I'm sure you've seen this with the big names. If you're good at attracting people to your message but don't feel like it's the right thing to offer a signature program, this could be a good option for you.

3.   **Investments:** Find an advisor you jive with, and let their energy manage it. One of the best financial lessons is the power of compound interest. Set a regular withdrawal, and forget about it, even if it's a small amount. Don't watch and worry about it all the time. You access it later, and it will need time to grow. Unlike property, this type of investment is usually liquid unless the fund is locked for some reason, usually tax reasons. Your advisor should help you figure out your risk tolerance and choose an investment right for you.

4.   **Income property:** Property has its own energy. So do renters. If this is an option for you, think about the logistics of the property you purchase. Are you OK with the occasional sounds, smells, and sharing of outdoor space of renting out a basement apartment? Suppose you don't live at the property. Are you willing to hire someone to manage it or be available yourself for the emergencies and maintenance that come up, usually at inconvenient times? You can rent rooms or suites via Airbnb or similar sites to earn cash and not have the long-term renter situation, but then the turnover presents another thing to manage. Another way property can make you money is by living in a place long enough to give you equity. You only access equity when you sell your home but typically re-invest it in another place to live. Equity isn't really the type of money you can rely on to provide stability unless you're willing to sell your property.

Managing your money is an integral part of business. Reducing the emotional reactivity around it is typically the first and most important step. The majority of what I do is help people manage the emotional roller coaster of business in my small group and 1:1 containers. Find out more here: **http://carmenfarrellknapp.com/workwithme**. You also want to think of ways to use your money to serve and support you rather than being at its mercy.

Signing off and a few CTA's

I have other books in this series that are the bomb once you use your strategy and authority consistently. The logical next step is the book in this series "Finding your Business Mojo with Human Design." This is where I really dive into leveraging your unique energy in your messaging and marketing. For example, where to look in your chart on who you might be best positioned to serve, how you best communicate, and how to use it to create your messaging.

Obvi, you can find me on social media. Handles change, but my name won't, so you can search me out as Carmen Farrell Knapp. I would love to hang out with you in the online world. Let me know how you're using Human Design in your business.

ABOUT THE AUTHOR

Hi there! I'm Carmen. I'm a serial entrepreneur, teacher, writer and coach. I have tons of formal and informal learning in energetic healing, adult education, coaching, quantum physics and a couple of decades of entrepreneurship.

Energetically I'm a 3-5 Manifesting Generator with the Incarnation Cross of the Vessel of Love. I live in Ontario, Canada with my partner Jeff, Basset Hound Roz and cat Dean.

I offer coaching programs, and courses in Human Design and business at www.carmenfarrellknapp.com

Printed in Great Britain
by Amazon

86190391R00122